At Home with Jesus

At Home with Jesus

Devotions for Children

Joslyn Wiechmann Moldstad

Illustrated By
Pastor Don Moldstad

NORTHWESTERN PUBLISHING HOUSE
Milwaukee, Wisconsin

Library of Congress Card 06N0691
Northwestern Publishing House
1250 N. 113th St., Milwaukee, WI 53226-3284
© 1992 by Northwestern Publishing House
Printed in the United States of America
ISBN 0-8100-0428-3

At Home with Jesus is dedicated
to my husband John
and to our children:

Rachel Renee
John Andrew
Matthew James
Michael John
Andrea Elizabeth
Joshua Ryan

Preface

Our home is a place of refuge to which we come each evening to be with our family. Every day is bursting with its own frustrations, heartaches, and grief. To be a real refuge, our home must be a place where we run not only for rest and relaxation, but also to hear the word of God. Only through the Bible is there true peace for our souls, knowing our sin is forgiven through Jesus the Savior.

Children also look forward to this time of peace as the family gathers about the word of God. *At Home with Jesus* is a devotional book especially for children between the ages of 5 and 13. Each devotion is based on a Bible passage from the New International Version and is in story form to spark children's interest.

One year in the life of the Anderson family is interwoven into 97 devotions. The children in this Christian family are: Lindsay, age 14; Jason, age 12; the twins Michael and Melissa, age 9; and Tracy, age 5. They experience problems and situations similar to those your own children may face.

Each Christ-centered devotion reminds us of our own sins and our need for a Savior. Through these Bible-based devotions your children will gain the courage to face their problems and will come to realize that God is always by their side to help them through all the troubles of life.

Joslyn Wiechmann Moldstad

Table of Contents

The Smallest Of Price Tags, The Greatest Of Gifts........2
Too Earthly? 5
Afraid Of Nothin' 7
Sunday-Morning-Go-To-Church...................................9
I'm Sorry, I'm Sorry 11
Beauty: More Than Skin Deep....................................13
God Demands One Hundred Percent 15
Pesky Flies 17
God Says...19
Troubles On Every Side, But Still There Is Peace........21
Suicide: A Lack Of Trust 23
Great In God's Kingdom 26
A Valentine Passage 28
Create In Me A Clean Heart, O God! 30
Fearless As A Child 32
Ice Palace 34
Adding Or Subtracting From God's Word?....................37
It Hurts 39
I Will Never Leave You..41
Honesty, Even To The Last Penny 43
Just Yes Or No 45
Happy With What I Am 47
When I Am Weak, That's When I'm Strong 50
First, You've Got To Hear The Bad News......................52
Obeying All The Time..54
Room For One More 56
True Wisdom 58
One Sin..60
God's Whipping Boy...62
Jesus Christ Died For All...64
How Much Did You Cost? 66
Particular 68

He's My Brother..70

Sloppy Work!...72

He's So Bad! 74

Just Because He Loves Me..76

Practice Makes Perfect...79

God's Recipes 81

Not By Ourselves...83

Zap It, Lord 85

I Had This Dream..87

Vacation From God's Word? 89

I'm Sorry, I Believe 91

Losing Sight Of Purpose 93

In Peace Or In Punishment?..95

A Happy Ending 97

I Am So Bored...100

I Don't Have To; I Want To 102

Our Journey Through Life 104

The Right Kind Of Sorrow 106

God Who Is The "Alls" 108

What A Friend We Have In Jesus 110

Wake Up! I Hear You Snoring!.......................................112

Why Work So Hard? 115

Being A Real Follower Of Jesus......................................117

The Lesson Of The Sunflower 118

Tomorrow May Be Too Late 120

Only What's Best For Me 122

Looking For Trouble?..124

Comfort, Comfort...125

Love Your Enemies 127

Inside Courage...130

Like A Soft Kitty..132

Better Half 134

It's Not Fair..136

Death Is Like A Swinging Door 139

I Wish I Was...141

Passing The Buck 143

Never Enough 145
Shipshape...147
Yes 149
Shout It From The Mountain Tops 151
That Old Wagging Tongue..153
Putting Out The Welcome Mat 155
Afraid To Share? 157
What Is Real?..159
When Forgiving Comes Hard......................................161
Short Fuse..164
A Little Exercise 166
Our Judge, Loving, But Fair...168
What Is Really Valuable? 170
Why, God, Why?...171
Are You Stingy With God's Gifts? 173
God's Way Of Starting Over With Us 175
Our Talents—Bragged, Buried, Or Used?....................177
Getting Even...179
Except Jesus Christ And Him Crucified 180
The Heart Of Prayer..183
Your Gospel Statement..185
Like A Tower Of Babel 187
A Lesson Of The Plant 189
I'm So Worried 191
Thanksgiving Inventory...193
Songs Of Thankfulness And Praise............................195
Growing Out Of Christmas? 197
Sometimes I Get So Sick Of Cute! 199
The Best Birthday 201

The Smallest Of Price Tags, The Greatest Of Gifts

For you know the grace of our Lord Jesus Christ that though he was rich, yet for your sakes he became poor, so that you through his poverty might become rich. (2 Corinthians 8:9)

The house smelled of buttery Christmas cookies and pine needles as the Anderson family hurried in from the cold, home from the Christmas Eve service. While Jason ran to light the tree, Mom quickly set the apple cider on the stove, and Lindsay carefully carried the brightly decorated cake into the living room. The younger children gathered around the tree, filling the room with squeals and giggles.

Two hours later the colorful wrappings were scattered among trails of ribbons and bows. The Christmas carols which had been sung earlier and the laughter which rang through the house, as each treasure was opened, still seemed to echo throughout the room. Mr. Anderson stood in the kitchen with two screws clamped tightly between his teeth, fastening a miniature blackboard to the wall. Tracy's eyes danced merrily as each tiny screw found its way home.

"Oh, Daddy!" she cried when the tiny blackboard was in place. She squeezed his leg and bubbled excitedly, "You're the greatest!"

Dad picked up his daughter and laughed merrily. "So, I am the greatest, am I? Well, if that doesn't beat all! For just one dollar and seventy-five cents, I can be the greatest! Little Tracy, you've certainly taught your daddy a valuable lesson!"

What valuable lesson had Mr. Anderson learned that night? Aunts, Uncles, Grandmas and Grandpas had showered the children with gifts, and Dad's own wallet was still recovering from the shock of Christmas shopping. The room was littered with an expensive train set, a whole family of dolls, and enough games to put the nearest toy store to shame. But here stood little Tracy, still humming a Christmas carol as she played with the most inexpensive toy in the house! That night Tracy taught her Dad never to judge a gift by its price tag.

Do you judge a gift by its price tag? On the outside, God's gift to you this Christmas doesn't look all that valuable. Jesus was born in a stable with farm animals all around him, not in a golden palace with house attendants waiting on his every need. No servants were there to test his bath water, wind his baby chimes, or fluff his royal bed pillow. Instead, this King of kings, was wrapped in rags and laid to rest on a bed of straw. The world did not realize what a treasure laid in that crude manger bed. There was no parade to honor him. There was no praise from the mighty of the world.

Why was Jesus born under such humble circumstances? God wanted us to know that his Son didn't come just for the rich and important, but also for the poor and the lowly. Jesus came for you. Jesus came for me. Jesus came to take away everything that is wrong with all of us: our uncaring spirits, our coldness, our hatred, our biting tongues, our blackest thoughts, our shame, our inability to love. He came to take away our sins.

The gift with the poorest of wrapping has made us the richest of all people. As you grow older, may you never lose sight of who Jesus really is. He remains the richest gift you possess because forgiveness of sins and life in heaven are found in him alone. Jesus, your Savior, is the most precious gift of all!

Prayer: Dear Jesus, forgive me when I forget how precious you are. Show me how I can never be truly happy only with things bought from a store. I need you, oh, my eternal and blessed God. Amen.

Too Earthly?

So whether you eat or drink or whatever you do, do it all for the glory of God. (1 Corinthians 10:31)

"Lindsay," Mom called from the kitchen. "I'm ready to frost the Christmas cookies. Want to help?"

Lindsay stopped her piano playing. For a moment her eyes danced with excitement. Suddenly, however, her brows curled into a puzzled frown. She hesitated. "No," she answered, "Let Melissa frost my share. She enjoys it so."

Mom stood at the door of the piano room, holding the frosting spoon in one hand and the bowl in the other. "But you enjoy decorating cookies more than anyone else!" Mom exclaimed. "I don't understand you. Yesterday you let Michael help me wrap presents, and you usually like to do that. The day before, you told Jason he could address the Christmas cards without you. Next thing I know you'll let someone decorate your share of the Christmas tree!"

Lindsay smiled, shrugging her shoulders slightly. "I do enjoy all the preparations at Christmas time, but I'm afraid I may enjoy them all a little too much. Ever since our religion teacher talked to us about how it's so easy to miss the real reason for celebrating Christmas, I decided to concentrate totally on Jesus and his birth. Doing all these other things is just too earthly. I'm afraid they will get in the way of really getting my heart ready for Jesus' birthday."

Mrs. Anderson smiled. "I wish everyone was so concerned about putting Christ first in their hearts. Its true. Too often people buy gifts, make cookies, and decorate a tree just for the sake of the fun involved. While Christians make these same types of preparations, they do so because they love and trust in Jesus as their Lord and Savior. Because they love him, they want to get ready for his birthday so they can honor him."

"Do you mean I don't have to feel guilty about getting excited over baking cookies, writing out cards, decorating the tree, and wrapping presents?" Lindsay asked.

"No, God doesn't want us to feel guilty. Rather, he wants our hearts to overflow with thankfulness for his many blessings. Helping a needy family with food and gifts, bringing a child to Sunday School, and including a scripture verse in a card are also important ways we can show that our celebration truly comes from our love for Jesus," Mom explained.

The way we celebrate Christmas and the way the world celebrates may sometimes look exactly alike. The difference can be found in our hearts. While the cards, presents, and decorations are the main parts of the celebration in many homes, in our homes the tree and decorations play only a small role. We rejoice in the gift God gave us in his Son Jesus. We celebrate *his* birthday. And in celebrating his birthday, we do all these things to show our love to him and to one another.

At Christmas then, let us come before the Lord with hearts that are thankful for the blessings we have of home and family. But let us especially be thankful for our Savior who lived, died, and rose again to set us free from all our sins. May God bless your thankful Christmas as you share this good news with others.

Prayer: Heavenly Father, this Christmas fill my heart with love and thankfulness for the gift to me of your Son Jesus. Amen.

Afraid Of Nothin'

Do not be afraid of those who kill the body but cannot kill the soul. Rather, be afraid of the One who can destroy both soul and body in hell. **(Matthew 10:28)**

Michael dug his hands deeply into his pockets as he trudged up the front sidewalk. He wore a scowl on his face that even the warm sun couldn't brighten. Jason, his brother, stood on the front porch holding the door open. "Chicken!" he shouted.

Michael's eyes, which had been silently counting the cracks in the sidewalk, flew upward and flared like angry flames. With one giant leap he flung his body up the porch steps, tackled his older brother, and began to pummel his stomach with his small, tight fists.

"Stop, would ya?" Jason yelled. "What's the matter with you?"

"No one calls me chicken and gets away with it!" Michael screamed.

"I didn't call *you* chicken," Jason cried in surprise. "I was talking to Lindsay. She had just asked me what we were having for supper, and I was trying to tell her that Mom was frying chicken!"

Michael relaxed instantly. Feeling rather foolish, he slumped backward. "You mean you weren't calling me names?"

"Of course not," Jason answered, shaking his head. "The next time Mom decides to fix chicken, I'll talk her out of it. You take it personally!"

A weak grin washed over Michael's face. "Boy do I feel dumb. But, you know, Cal Vance has been calling me chicken because I won't swim the canal with him."

"Are you going to jump into a polar bear's cage every time someone questions your bravery?" asked Jason.

"Do you mean like those three boys from Brooklyn did a while back when someone dared them to climb into the bear's cage?" Michael asked.

Jason nodded. "They saw that dare as a real test of their

bravery. But look what happened. One boy was mauled to death, and the other two will relive that horrible tragedy for the rest of their lives. The worst part is that the boy's death was meaningless. It didn't have to happen. It was a waste of the life God had given him."

"Isn't there any way a guy can prove his bravery without doing something foolish like that? asked Michael.

"Well, sure. He can stand up for what he believes even when people make fun of him. Noah had that kind of courage. In a world filled with wickedness, he walked with God. He wasn't afraid to preach against the wickedness of the world and live the way God wanted him to. He kept his faith in the true God when no one else had time for him. I can almost hear the names they called him as he was constructing the ark God told him to build."

"Sometimes it takes more courage to be called chicken and to do what is right than to go along with sinning," Jason answered.

"A really brave person wouldn't use illegal drugs just to make friends. He wouldn't cheat on tests, disobey his parents, or lie just to prove he's tough around the other guys," Michael reasoned.

"A really brave person would let others know when they sin and how much they need a Savior. He might even bring another person to church."

Michael's eyes grew wide. "Being brave doesn't always mean you have to take risks. Asking a guy like Cal to church would be as hard as swimming the canal 100 times."

"Maybe harder," Jason answered, "but with so much more meaning."

Prayer: Dear Lord Jesus, sometimes I feel I have to show off my courage by taking foolish risks. I am sorry for this. Please give me a strong faith to stand up for what I believe. Amen.

Sunday-Morning-Go-To-Church

Blessed are those who hunger and thirst for righteousness, for they will be filled. (Matthew 5:6)

Melissa opened one eye and looked at the clock. She coughed. Perhaps she was just too sick to go to church. She wiggled her toes. Ouch! The ankle she had fallen on while roller skating still throbbed. Melissa rolled over. The clothes closet came into view. Oops! There lay her best Sunday dress crumpled on the floor of her closet. A cough, a throbbing ankle, a rumpled dress—not one but three reasons it would be impossible to go to church today.

A loud moan interrupted Melissa's thoughts. She turned her head toward the bed beside hers. Lindsay's eyes were closed tightly, but her arms thrashed about vigorously. Her fists were clenched as if she were experiencing great pain.

"Lindsay! Lindsay!" Melissa called, shaking her older sister's arm. "Wake up! Wake up! It's just a dream. You're in bed. It's Sunday morning."

Lindsay blinked at her sister. "Sunday morning?" She rubbed her blanket. "The day we go to church?"

"Of course, silly! We always go to church on Sunday! You sound as if you haven't gone in months!"

"After what happened in my dream, it seems like years," Lindsay answered. "My dream was so real. I was a prisoner in a concentration camp."

"Why, what had you done?" asked Melissa.

"I don't remember that. I just remember how awful the concentration camp was. I was in a tiny cell with no windows. I had to sleep on the floor without any blankets. My only food was a raw potato and a tin of water once a day."

"What did you do?" Melissa asked, gripping her own blanket tightly.

"There was nothing *to* do. I couldn't get out. I was desperate. Then one day I heard a voice speaking to me from the next cell."

"What was the voice saying? Was someone trying to rescue you?"

"Yes, in a way another prisoner *was* trying to rescue me. Her whisper was really faint, but the words kept coming. This is what I heard: 'For the Lamb at the center of the throne will be their shepherd; he will lead them to springs of living water. And God will wipe away every tear from their eyes.' "

"That's a passage from the book of Revelation," Melissa observed. "Isn't it?"

"Yes, Revelation 7:17. But the voice didn't know just that one passage; she knew hundreds of them."

"I began to forget how lonely and sad I felt," Lindsay said. "Even in a prison cell, I knew Jesus was there with me and no one could take Christ and his cross away from me. I knew that even if I died there, I'd be taken to heaven."

"Girls! Girls!" Lindsay and Melissa heard their mother call from the kitchen. "Hurry and get dressed or we'll be late for church."

Melissa and Lindsay bolted from their beds, stumbling and tripping on their way into the bathroom. "Did you ever feel almost hungry to go to church?" asked Lindsay.

"Yes, right now!" Melissa giggled. Somehow the cough, sore ankle, and rumpled dress had long been forgotten. "Maybe too many comforts make us forget how important and wonderful God's word is! I mean, think of its power to bring hope even to a dirty prison cell!"

"I know!" Lindsay answered triumphantly. "I've been there!"

Prayer: Dear Savior, forgive me for taking the hearing of your word for granted. Help me to hunger and thirst after your goodness. There is no other comfort that can satisfy my soul. I need your forgiveness. Amen.

I'm Sorry, I'm Sorry

Have mercy on me, O God, according to your unfailing love; according to your great compassion blot out my transgressions. **(Psalm 51:1)**

Melissa Anderson sat at her desk carefully snipping colorful pieces of construction paper into various sizes. "Melissa!" a voice called from behind. "That's the paper I bought for my science project. Now you've used it all!"

"Sorry, Michael," Melissa said lightly, trying to soothe his anger.

Later that afternoon, Lindsay wanted to play her favorite record album. As she was about to set the record on the turntable, she cried out. "My brand new needle is broken!" She stared angrily at her younger sister. "Melissa, did you do this?"

"Sorry," Melissa replied casually, turning the pages of her book.

In the early evening Jason was carefully sketching a still life of oranges and apples he had set into an old cracked bowl. Melissa bumped his arm, sending a black line shooting across his picture.

"Sorry," Melissa exclaimed as Jason cried out in surprise. She reached for one of the apples in the bowl and took a bite out of it.

"Melissa! You've ruined my scene," Jason exclaimed, trying to rub away the offending line. "Put that apple back. You have no feelings."

"I said I was sorry," Melissa muttered defiantly.

"Sure, you are about as sorry as you were about using up all my paper or about breaking Lindsay's new stereo needle," Michael said.

Melissa's eyes filled with tears. "You won't even believe a person when she says she's sorry!" she moaned.

"We're just wondering if you really *are* sorry!" Lindsay answered. "You knew that paper was Michael's, and you

11

know that you are supposed to leave my stereo alone."

"And you could see I was drawing," Jason blurted out, as he stared sadly at his ruined picture.

"You say you are sorry like Big Barney Thompson does as he pushes his way through a crowded bus," Michael piped in. "From the front to the back he averages ten 'I'm sorrys' as he clumsily plows his way through. He doesn't care how many toes he steps on. He just says he is sorry and expects the kids to understand. Well, nobody is fooled or thinks he's really sorry at all. It's just some words he uses to get him through the bus."

Melissa slowly walked over to Dad who had been sitting in the living room chair listening. "Dad," she asked meekly. "Are my 'I'm sorrys' like Big Barney's?"

Mr. Anderson pulled his young daughter up on his lap. "We're all guilty sometimes of sounding like Big Barney, Melissa. Real apologies come from a truly sad heart, one that's truly sorry for any wrong it's done. We aren't truly sorry if we plan to do wrong and then think that we can quickly say those two magic words—even if we don't mean them—and expect everything to be okay."

"What should I say then?" asked Melissa.

"Saying those words is good, but we should also feel them in our hearts. When we say 'I'm sorry,' it's as if we were telling another person that we'd act differently if we would actually have a chance to do it all over again."

"When we sin against another person, we have also sinned against God," Mom continued. "In the Bible, God tells us he won't turn away our apologies if they come from a sad and broken heart."

"Only God can look into our hearts and see if we are *truly* sorry about our sin. Think of the thief on the cross. Jesus knew he was truly repentant of all his sins and that he trusted in Jesus' mercy to save him. It wasn't a Big Barney's 'I'm sorry,' but God saw genuine sorrow in his heart."

Melissa nodded and left the room. In a few minutes she

returned with her bank. She pressed a few dollars into both Lindsay's and Michael's hands. "I don't have enough to buy a whole new needle," she told her sister, "but I'll start saving." She turned to Jason. "I can't redo your picture. But I am really sorry. Not a Big Barney's sorry, but a Melissa Anderson's sorry!"

Prayer: Dear Jesus, help me to feel true sadness and sorrow when I hurt someone. Lead me to confess my sin and seek your forgiveness. In your name I pray. Amen.

Beauty: More Than Skin Deep

Your beauty should not come from outward adornment, such as braided hair and the wearing of gold jewelry and fine clothes. Instead, it should be that of your inner self, the unfading beauty of a gentle and quiet spirit, which is of great worth in God's sight. (1 Peter 3:3,4)

Lindsay Anderson was already eating her morning cereal when Mom hurried into the kitchen to get the school lunches ready. "You certainly woke up with the birds today, Lindsay!" Mom greeted her. "Are you meeting your friends early at the Senior High?"

Lindsay nodded, but she didn't look up from her cereal bowl. Mrs. Anderson continued to chat with her daughter while she carefully spread the bread with peanut butter and jelly. Every question she asked Lindsay was answered with a nod or quiet reply.

"You must have added too much honey to that new cereal." Mom laughed, "It really has you glued to the bowl!" Mrs. Anderson reached over and gently raised her daughter's chin. As she peered into Lindsay's face, her smile quickly turned to a look of surprise.

"Lindsay, what have you done to your face?" she asked. "Are those false eyelashes?" Mrs. Anderson pulled up a chair beside Lindsay and surveyed the heavy makeup, eyeliner, eyebrow pencil, thick lipstick, and bright red blush.

"I was afraid you wouldn't approve," Lindsay responded anxiously. "But all the girls my age wear makeup. You don't want me to be the only pale face in Senior High, do you, Mom? Boys will never notice me!"

"Oh, Lindsay, I do think it's important to look nice, but I think overdoing the makeup will give boys a different kind of message."

"Do you mean they might think I'm just a run-around?"

"They might," Mom answered. "Of course, I'm not against using a little makeup. I wear it too. But makeup shouldn't hide the main attraction. In the Bible God reminds us that our true beauty shouldn't be found just on the outside. Real beauty is an 'unfading beauty of a quiet and gentle spirit.'"

"But if I keep too quiet I'll be a plain wallflower. Not even the girls will notice me!" Lindsay complained.

"Please don't misunderstand me, dear. God isn't saying we shouldn't talk and converse. He doesn't want us to be bores either. But our whole personality and how we dress and how we behave should show how much we love Jesus. It should show others we really care about the important things in life."

Like Lindsay's mother, your parents surely never want to downplay the importance of keeping a neat appearance. God doesn't want his children to look as if they've just walked through a pigsty, not caring how they look. But beauty is more than skin deep, and nothing is more beautiful to God than a young person who lives and acts as his child.

How much more beautiful is a person who speaks kind words instead of angry or indecent language. How much more attractive we appear to others when we take the time to cheer up someone rather than to run them into the ground with our gossip. More important than fancy, expensive clothing and a well made-up face is a countenance which radiates the love we have for Jesus.

Every Christian makeup kit should include the most important ingredient necessary to develop such inner beauty. This ingredient is God's word. Only if we continually use God's word will the love and respect we have for Jesus be displayed in our personality. Only then will our beauty be more than skin deep.

Prayer: Dear Jesus, forgive me for trying to obtain true beauty from expensive clothes and makeup. Remind me constantly of your loving death on the cross to pay for my sins, and then remind me of your glorious resurrection. Let my way of living show others that I truly belong to you. Amen.

God Demands One Hundred Percent

For whoever keeps the whole law and yet stumbles at just one point is guilty of breaking all of it. (James 2:10)

"Michael! Come in here!" Mr. Anderson called sternly.

"What's the matter?" asked Michael, running in from the front porch.

"Have you seen your report card?" asked Dad.

Michael nodded ashamedly. "Were you looking at my spelling grade?"

"Yes," Dad answered. "I don't see how anyone could fail spelling! Last year you had nothing but A's in spelling."

"It's really not fair, Dad! Miss Kasten has a rule that if you don't get 100%, every word spelled perfectly, your grade is an automatic F!"

Melissa nodded. "It's true, Dad. Most of Michael's tests had only one or two mistakes on them. But it doesn't matter to Miss Kasten. One wrong is the same as getting them all wrong!"

The Anderson twins were frustrated about the way their teacher graded spelling tests. After all, no one is perfect. Yet, Miss Kasten demanded 100% from her students.

God also demands 100% from us! He wants us to be perfect, to keep the law perfectly. We might compare the law to a windowpane. When it is hit by a ball, it shatters entirely. Likewise, to break the law in one point makes us guilty of breaking all of it. Breaking even one commandment of God makes us sinners and makes us guilty before God. We deserve to be sentenced to hell, for the wages of sin is death, eternal death.

Many people think God could never be so harsh, so demanding. They feel that if they do their best, God will let at least a few of their sins slip by.

Trying our best, however, won't erase the sins we've already committed. Even before we could try to do our best, we had a black mark against us. Since our parents are sinful, we too are sinful. And God tells us in his word that he demands perfection. He is holy and just. He must punish sin.

How thankful we are that God is loving and merciful as well as just. Jesus lived a perfect life in our place and paid for our sins on the cross. He satisfied his Father's justice. Since we believe, we are saved through Jesus' holy precious blood. God pronounces us forgiven. Through Jesus our grade for this life is 100%—A plus!

It is a losing battle to try to win heaven for ourselves by

doing good. Heaven is ours only through Jesus' perfection. Now our life can be lived fearlessly, doing good, not to obtain heaven, but in thankfulness to God for being merciful, as well as just!

Prayer: Dear Father in Heaven, please forgive all of my sins for Jesus' sake. Thank you for marking Jesus' perfect score on my report card. Serving you is no longer a chore, but my joy. Amen.

Pesky Flies

Be self-controlled and alert. Your enemy the devil prowls around like a roaring lion looking for someone to devour. (1 Peter 5:8)

"Quick, Jason, get that lion before he bites you," cried little Jeffie Maas.

Puzzled, Jason looked up from his notebook. "What's Jeffie talking about? Doesn't he know the difference between a lion and a fly?" he asked Lindsay.

"He calls flies 'lions' because he's deathly afraid of them. He doesn't like the way they swoop down and sit on him."

"Nothing's more harmless than a fly," Jason told Jeffie.

"Well, the common housefly may look harmless, but did you know one fly can carry up to 63 different diseases at one time?" Lindsay's eyes darted around the room. "As a matter-of-fact, your room is crawling with them. I hope you aren't starting a collection."

Jason grinned. "Michael opened the window without the screen. That's the way they got in. But don't worry. When I find the time, I'll swat a few."

Several days later, Lindsay was surprised to see her brother sick in bed. He feebly grunted hello as Lindsay sat down beside him. "You were right about those flies, Lindsay, they did me in. My head is stuffed up. My throat is scratchy. I'm achy all over. I wish I'd have been smart like you and swatted them away while I had the chance."

"Oh, I'm not so smart either," Lindsay sighed. "I have a few innocent looking flies in my own life that I haven't gotten rid of either."

Jason looked puzzled. "Flies, as in the swatting kind?"

Lindsay smiled. "No, the flies bothering me are the *seemingly* harmless words and ideas floating around, trying to pull me away from Jesus."

"In books I find bad language, even from some very interesting authors," Lindsay continued to explain. "In music I find talk about drugs and sex, even in really catchy melodies. Among some of my really close friends I find that some want to drink, some want to disobey their parents, and some want to lie and cheat. In TV shows I find dirty jokes, bad language—all of the above!"

Jason nodded. "I think I understand you now. A little bad language, a movie that is just a tiny bit sexy, music which says drugs aren't so bad—they are all like flies. They make us begin to think that a little bit of sin isn't so bad."

"But just as a tiny fly can give you a germ to make your body sick, bad influences can weaken your faith in Jesus. And pretty soon sin just doesn't seem to shock you like it used to."

"A person should never think he is strong enough to say no to temptation," Jason added. "It's much safer to push the temptation away, just like a person would swat a fly."

"I've learned some of the most innocent looking pleasures can turn out to be roaring lions," Lindsay said.

Jason propped himself up on one elbow. "Lindsay, tell little Jeffie Maas he can keep calling flies 'lions'. For as sick as they make me feel, it's best not to get too friendly with them. And when I'm feeling better, I think I'll go through my tapes and books to see if I have a few of my own 'lions' slinking around."

18

Prayer: Dear Jesus, forgive me for sometimes thinking that a little bit of sin is not harmful to my soul. Give me strength to push away these pesky flies, to fight against the devil's temptations. Amen.

God Says

He who listens to you listens to me; he who rejects you rejects me; but he who rejects me rejects him who sent me. (Luke 10:16)

Michael sat in the damp basement bending patiently over his wood set. Jason called from the top step, "Dad says to come and give him a hand in the garage."

Michael glanced up from his work. "Tell him I'm busy now," he answered.

A few minutes later Melissa clip-clopped down the basement steps. "Michael!" she spoke sternly. "Didn't you hear? Daddy says to come into the garage, now!" she exclaimed.

Michael frowned. "I told Jason I can't leave this now, and

I'll tell you the same," he replied saucily. "If Dad wants me, he can very well come down himself and get me."

The basement seemed to fall into a cold damp silence as two heavy feet slowly and deliberately plodded down the steps. "Dad is here!" Mr. Anderson thundered sternly. "Why didn't you come when I called?"

The blood drained from Michael's face as he rushed to get to his feet. Quickly he scrambled up the staircase, forgetting his proud and cocky attitude.

Michael remembered that day for a long time afterward. He learned to respond quickly to the words, "Dad says," knowing that he would have to pay the consequences if he didn't.

At a very young age, you also learned to respond to the words "Dad says" or "Mom says." Whether you respond out of love for your parents or out of fear of punishment, you do what your parents ask. Out of an even greater respect and love for him, God wants us to respond to what he says.

Just as Mr. Anderson sent his son and daughter to call Michael to him, so God, our heavenly Father, sends pastors, parents, and teachers to proclaim his wishes to us. When parents encourage us to be honest and hard-working children, we should respond just as if God himself were talking to us. When teachers and pastors encourage us to be faithful in our studies and in our hearing of God's word, God wants us to listen.

Poor Michael forgot that if he didn't obey what his sister and brother said, his father himself was sure to come and make his son obey. To see his father's angry eyes frowning down on him left him with a terrible feeling. How much more frightening it will be for us to see God's angry eyes, if we haven't listened to those he has placed over us.

We all have sinned many times in our lives. Should we then be afraid of God's coming on Judgment Day? We don't have to be. We can be assured that God will be looking at us with kind and forgiving eyes, if we feel sorry for our sins and believe they have been forgiven through Christ. Then for Christ's sake, on Judgment Day God will appear as a loving Father instead of an angry judge.

Knowing we are forgiven, we will gladly listen to those whom God has placed over us. We understand that growing into faithful, believing adults is our way of saying "thank you" to God who has shown us so much mercy.

Prayer: Dear Jesus, forgive me when I'm disobedient to those you have placed over me. Remind me that my parents, pastor, and teachers are only carrying out your commands. Help me, out of love for you, to do what they say. Amen.

Troubles On Every Side, But Still There Is Peace

Peace I leave with you; my peace I give you. I do not give to you as the world gives. Do not let your hearts be troubled and do not be afraid. (John 14:27)

The Anderson children crowded around the little bundle, securely wrapped in Mom's loving arms. The tiny baby, so small, so delicate, slept quietly.

"He looks so peaceful," Melissa whispered. "How can he sleep so quietly knowing his mother and father are dead?" she moaned.

Michael nudged his twin sister. "Little Justin doesn't know his parents are dead. He's so little. How could he know they died in a car crash?"

"But as he gets older, we'll have to tell him what happened," Tracy interrupted. "The tears will just roll down his little cheeks when he finds out he's an orphan."

He'll never sleep so peacefully again," Melissa added.

"Oh, I think he will," Mom answered. "You are forgetting that Aunt Carol and Uncle Bill had little Justin baptized when he was born. He won't have to worry about how he'll get to heaven. He won't have to worry about making up for his sins. They've all been forgiven through Jesus' blood on the cross."

"What about the fact that he's an orphan? Won't that ever bother him?" asked Jason.

"I'm sure he'll be sad that he never really knew or talked to his parents," Dad explained, "but all parents have to die some time."

"They do?" asked little Tracy. She had never thought about that.

"Yes," Mom answered solemnly. "We hope and pray no child loses his parents, as little Justin did, before he is full grown. But whatever happens, the peace of knowing his sins are forgiven through Jesus will always be his."

"God's peace isn't like the world's," Dad broke in. "What happens when two kings or two presidents sit down together at a table and talk about ending the war between their countries and establishing peace?"

"Well, they draw up a treaty," Jason answered. "A treaty is a promise not to fight each other."

"But sometimes—even before the ink is barely dry—what can happen to that treaty they've just signed?" asked Dad.

"The peace treaty can be broken. One king may decide he'd rather fight his enemy than have peace."

"The peace treaty God has made with us is so different," Mom continued. "It can never be broken. Once God promises to forgive sins, he can't go back on his word. His treaty with us stands forever."

"It's impossible for that treaty to be broken because it's

been signed in blood!" Lindsay replied.

"Yes, with the blood Jesus spilled while dying on the cross, the peace treaty between God and man was signed for eternity."

"The world could never promise God's kind of peace," Jason added, "because people like Justin's parents die, and there are wars, and people get sick, and they go hungry, and they lose everything in floods, and . . . and . . . and there are all kinds of disasters."

Mom squeezed little Justin tightly and nodded. "Yes, a terrible thing happened when Justin's parents died. And who knows what other sorrows this little baby will have to face in his lifetime? But the important thing to remember is that whatever happens to him, he can always have peace."

"True peace in Jesus, his Savior," Tracy added with a smile.

Prayer: Dear Jesus, these days everyone is talking about peace. Help us all to realize we can have no peace without you and the forgiveness of our sins. Only in you is there true peace. Amen.

Suicide: A Lack of Trust

In him we have redemption through his blood, the forgiveness of sins. (Ephesians 1:7)

"What are you doing your term paper on, Lindsay?" asked Grandma Anderson.

Lindsay sat at her grandmother's old oak table munching cookies. "I'm writing about why people commit suicide. Have you ever known anyone who took his own life?"

Grandma nodded solemnly. "I was only seven when I learned how ugly suicide could be. I was coming home from our old country school house, and I took a shortcut through our neighbor's pasture. Off in the distance I could see Mrs. Elliot and her two little girls coming toward me through the field. I thought it was sort of strange that they were dressed up in their Sunday best when it was only Wednesday. I waved and yelled hello, but Mrs. Elliot pretended she didn't hear me."

"There was an old well next to a deserted farmhouse on their property. They headed straight for it. When they got there, Mrs. Elliot hesitated only a moment, and then she took those two lovely little girls and pushed them over the side into that deep well. Then she jumped in after them."

"Oh, Grandma, did you run for help?"

"Like a jack-rabbit I ran!" Grandma answered excitedly, "but by the time my dad and Mr. Elliot got there it was too late. The well was very deep, and it was practically dry. They didn't drown. It was the terrible fall that killed all three of them."

"Why did she do it, Grandma? Why did she commit suicide?" Lindsay shivered "And to think she killed her little girls with her."

"No one ever found out for sure why she did it. Some said the family was deep in debt, and they were about to lose the farm. Others claimed her husband drank."

Lindsay pulled out a piece of note paper from a library book and set it on the table. "During study hall I jotted down a few other reasons why people kill themselves. Some are lonely or depressed from guilty feelings. One boy my age killed himself because he didn't get an A in math. Another girl ended it all because she didn't make the cheerleading squad."

"To us, these reasons seem really foolish," said Grandma, "but most, though not all, suicides come about because these people don't trust fully in Jesus for help with their problems."

"When someone is sad, I often hear folks say, 'Just look on the bright side,' or 'Things will look better in the morning.' "

Grandma nodded solemnly. "Often the tomorrows are just as bad as the todays. If we really want to help someone and cheer them up, we must realize that their main problem is sin. Mistakes we've made, sins we've committed, and the guilty feelings which follow are hard to live with. A favorite passage of mine, one that really helps me, is Ephesians 1:7, 'In him we have redemption through his blood, the forgiveness of sins.' "

"Do you mean that when people know their sins are forgiven, they can face all their other problems better?"

Grandma nodded. "When we know that heaven is ours through Jesus' suffering on the cross, it's much easier to bear the problems of this life. We know that some day the world will end, and all our problems will end with it."

"And when we believe that Jesus will take us to heaven where he rules over everything, then we also know he is strong enough to help us out of all of our other problems," Lindsay added.

Ending our own life in suicide is like slapping God in the face. He wants to carry our burdens for us and to put an end to our problems, but we are refusing to give him that opportunity.

So, no matter how difficult our problems become, no matter how hopeless our situation seems to be, let us learn to hand all of our problems over to Jesus when they become too hard for us to bear. He stretched his arms out on the cross to save us, and they are still reaching out to help us.

Prayer: Dear Jesus, help me always to respect the life you've given me. Help me to listen to those with troubles so I can help them by telling them how much you love them. Forgive all my sins, especially when I don't trust you enough. Amen.

Great In God's Kingdom

I have set you an example that you should do as I have done for you. (John 13:15)

Lindsay Anderson sadly fingered one of the menus she had prepared for the Valentine Sweetheart Dinner at church. "Here you are, girls! Ice cold lemonade for . . ." Mom's joyful announcement trailed off as she saw the nearly empty living room. "Where did your friends disappear to? Is your meeting over already?"

"We hit a little snag and everyone left in a huff," Lindsay explained.

"What kind of a snag?" asked Mom, picking up the committee list. "Posters and menus have been decided. Entertainment and cooks have been chosen. I do hate to see anything spoil the Sweetheart Dinner. It was such a delightful way to honor your parents."

"The problem is that no one wants to work the clean-up detail after the fun and food are over! Carol says if God had meant her to be a janitor, he would have given her bigger hands. Sandy says scraping dirty dishes will spoil her nails. Mark says doing dishes and washing tables are women's work!"

"Why don't *you* volunteer to be in charge of clean-up?" Mom suggested.

"Mom, I'm in charge of decorations. I shouldn't have to handle clean-up, too! I'm an artist, Mom. Should my talent be wasted sweeping floors and taking out garbage?"

"There's not much creativity in scraping plates, I suppose," Mom hesitated. "Yet, I do hate to see the whole dinner scrapped. I know," she brightened. "*I'll* head up your clean-up committee. The dinner and entertainment will be over by then, so I won't be missing a thing. After all, there's not a dish, table, or dirty floor too hard for these hands to tackle."

"Mom!" Lindsay protested. "You can't be in charge of clean-up!" The parents are the guests of honor. Do you want to spoil your pretty dress doing dishes?"

"If it'll bring a little peace to your group, I'll do it."

Lindsay stared at her mother for a long time. "You aren't joking, are you?"

Mom shook her head. "If Jesus could stop his disciples' bickering by washing their feet, I can wash a few tables and dry a few dishes."

"The disciples had been arguing about who was the greatest among them, weren't they?" asked Lindsay.

Mom nodded. "Jesus showed his disciples that it wasn't seeking places of honor which would make them great, but simply serving one another."

Ashamed, Lindsay bowed her head. "Even *I* thought I was too good to wash dishes!"

"It's hard for any of us to swallow our pride, but if the Son of God could humble himself enough to die a criminal's death on the cross in our place, how can any of us think any job or task is beneath our dignity?"

"I've never known anyone filled with so much love!" said Lindsay.

A few days later, Mom walked into the living room with a freshly-typed copy of the Sweetheart Dinner's program. "Lindsay, I'm afraid I've found an error here. Your name is printed under clean-up, not decoration."

"It's no error," Lindsay explained. "The artist swallowed a huge chunk of pride and volunteered for clean-up. The peculiar thing was that eight or nine others volunteered almost immediately. Do you suppose their mothers told them the story of how Jesus washed his disciples' feet, too?" she grinned.

"It is possible," Mom replied, "or your kindness could have melted their hearts into service, also."

Prayer: Dear Jesus, forgive me for often being too proud to do some jobs for which I think I'm too good. Help me in all humility to serve others even as you have served me in dying for my sins. Amen.

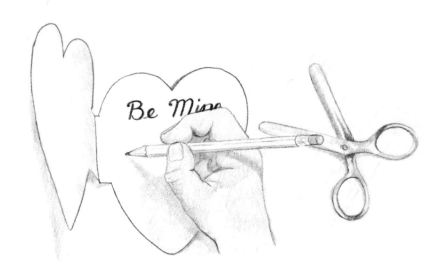

A Valentine Passage

For the wages of sin is death, but the gift of God is eternal life in Christ Jesus our Lord. **(Romans 6:23)**

Melissa and Michael were giggling loudly as they pushed the back door open. Their older brother Jason was already helping himself to the warm chocolate chip cookies setting on the counter.

"What's so funny?" asked Jason.

Melissa scrambled up beside her brother to help herself to the cookies, too. "We're making valentine cards in school for our parents. Miss Kasten suggested we write a Bible passage on the inside of our cards for the verse."

"We were supposed to pick a passage about God's love to us, because that is the best kind of love there is," Michael added.

"Well, Craig Thompson spent most of art class drawing hearts and cupids on the front of his card. At the last minute he needed a passage to write on the inside of his card," Melissa explained.

"He wanted to finish his card before the bell rang, but he couldn't think of a single passage except one. Do you know the passage he picked?" Michael's eyes were twinkling brightly. " 'The wages of sin is death.' Can you believe it, choosing that passage for a Valentine card?"

Both twins roared with laughter. "His card was supposed to make his parents feel happy," Melissa snickered. "They'll probably burst into tears the minute they read what he wrote!"

Mrs. Anderson had been listening to the conversation from the living room. As she came into the room and sat down beside the children, she couldn't hide the smile on her face. "You know, the passage Craig picked was really an excellent one."

"But, Mom, who wants to hear about a gloomy thing like death on Valentine's Day?" Michael asked.

"Let me finish," Mom said gently. "Craig picked the right passage, but he left the joyful part out."

Mom quickly flipped through the pages of the family Bible and showed the passage to the children. "The wages of sin is death, but the gift of God is eternal life in Christ Jesus our Lord."

Melissa looked surprised. "I never knew that passage had a happy ending!" she exclaimed.

Mom sipped her coffee and set the cup gently into its saucer. "You see, God's Word is filled with gloomy passages, or we usually call them law passages. These law passages show us our sins. They explain how we haven't kept God's commandments perfectly. But thanks to our loving God, the Bible also contains the gospel or joyful passages."

"The law and the gospel are both in this same passage!" exclaimed Jason.

"And we sinners need to hear both parts," Mom told them. "We need to hear how sinful we are. Not only do we deserve death in this life, but we also deserve eternal death in hell."

"After hearing how bad we are, it sure is great to hear there still is hope for us!" Michael cried.

"And that hope is found in the gospel. The gospel tells us our sins have been forgiven through Jesus," Mom continued.

"Tomorrow, I'll tell Craig he didn't spoil his card after all! I'll tell him he still can write in the very best part!" Melissa cried.

Prayer: Dear Jesus, thank you for giving me the law and the gospel in your word. Help me to remember to use both when I am telling others about you. For your sake, please forgive my many sins. Amen.

Create In Me A Clean Heart, O God!

But the things that come out of the mouth come from the heart, and these make a man "unclean." (Matthew 15:18)

The Anderson twins were sprawled out on the floor of the living room playing a game of checkers. "I think Miss Kasten should invest in a big roll of tape and plaster Timmy's mouth shut with it," Melissa told her brother.

"No, he'd have to take the tape off to eat," Michael answered. "I think she should use the biggest bar of soap she can find and suds up his mouth until he blows bubbles! That would teach him!"

Lindsay looked up from her book in wonderment. "I can't figure out whether you two want to strangle someone or do the wash!" she declared.

Melissa giggled softly. "We were just trying to think of some fool-proof method to stop Timmy Johnson from using bad language."

"In medieval times they used all sorts of strange punishments to keep a person from doing wrong. If you were caught stealing, they would punish you by chopping your hand off."

Melissa winced. "That sounds a little drastic to me."

"It was," Lindsay agreed, "and still it didn't always keep that thief or others from wanting what didn't belong to them. Cutting off hands or taping mouths isn't really getting to the root of the problem. In Timmy's case, Miss Kasten would have more success if she could reach his heart."

"Are you saying cursing and swearing begin in his heart, with his thoughts?" asked Michael. He thought for a moment. "You know, when Mom wants something really clean, she uses bleach. It used to work wonders on Tracy's diapers," he added.

"Except we don't want to poison Tim in the process," Lindsay chuckled. "No, it's the bleach bottle of God's word that Timmy needs to hear. First of all, Timmy needs to know why he should stop using bad language."

"If he'd just understand how sad Jesus is when he hears those words, it might keep him from using them," Melissa replied.

"If he would realize how much Jesus suffered on the cross to pay for his thoughtless words, I'm sure he'd feel sorry when one slips out!" Michael added.

Lindsay nodded "All of our sins come from the heart, and each of us, it seems, has one that is a little harder to fight against. For Timmy it's using bad language; for others it might be laziness or cheating or lying. We all need the bleach bottle of God's word to make us truly clean on the inside."

"Why is it easier to say no to the devil on some days than on other days?" Michael asked.

"Well, perhaps some days our faith isn't quite as strong as

on other days. Or it could be the devil is just working harder on certain days to make us sin. Jesus told his disciples in the garden of Gethsemane that it took watching and praying not to fall into temptation."

"That could be the reason Mom and Dad don't want us to skip devotions, even when we are in a hurry to go somewhere. They want us to be on our guard, always ready for the devil's tricks," Melissa replied thoughtfully.

"I wonder if Timmy's family would like to start regular family devotions," Michael said. "We could loan them one of our books to help them get started."

Melissa smiled. "It sure sounds a lot smarter than buying rolls of tape or bars of soap."

"And a lot more effective!" Lindsay grinned.

Prayer: Dear Jesus, wash me clean with your blood which you shed for me on the cross. I know my sin begins in my wicked heart. Keep me close to your word so I may remain truly clean, inside and out! Amen.

Fearless As A Child

Pray also for me, that whenever I open my mouth, words may be given me so that I will fearlessly make known the mystery of the gospel. (Ephesians 6:19)

"Did you girls enjoy your dinner with your piano teacher?" Mom asked her daughters when she heard the front door close.

Lindsay's answer came across the living room in a long, loud groan. "Lindsay says I spoiled the whole dinner," Melissa explained sadly.

"Such a lovely dinner, too!" Lindsay inserted. "Mrs. Larsen was dressed so elegantly, as she always is. She was wearing a beautiful white dress with a high collar. A pretty black bow was tied around her waist with sparkling buttons down the back. The outfit was stunning! But during the dinner Melissa blurted out, 'Did you put your dress on backwards?' I felt like crawling under the table from embarrassment."

"I didn't mean any harm," Melissa replied softly. "Her dress was so plain in the front and so fancy in the back. I was sure she had put it on wrong."

Lindsay rolled her eyes toward the ceiling, while Mom's eyes twinkled merrily with laughter. "You know, Lindsay, this reminds me of the time you asked Mrs. Whitmore why her hair kept changing color every week."

"Mom, I'd never say something so rude!" exclaimed Lindsay.

"Probably not now," Mom laughed, "but when you were Melissa's age, you were constantly spouting off with peculiar questions. You weren't trying to be cruel. You just wanted to know. That is just how children are."

"It's this same fearlessness in a child that makes her stand on one side of the street and yell across to a neighbor, 'Hey, do you believe in Jesus?' " Dad shared as he put the evening paper down. "When you were younger, Lindsay, you did that quite often."

"I did?" Lindsay gulped. Just then a frown formed between her eyes. Dad's words made her think. "Too bad I'm not so fearless any more," she answered. "Now, when I want to talk to someone about my Savior, I get all sweaty and choked up. Why am I so different now?"

"I think it is called growing up!" Dad smiled. "You no longer blurt out the first thought that crosses your mind. You think your words through and even anticipate how people will react. You realize that many people don't believe the Bible is truly God's word. Instead of feeling you can convince them of their need for a Savior, you are afraid that you may be laughed at."

Lindsay nodded. "Yet, I don't want to be afraid of talking about Jesus. How do I become fearless again?"

"We can become fearless only with God's help," Mom answered. "The apostle Paul also realized how much he needed courage, so he asked the believers at Ephesus to pray for him when he preached God's word."

Like the Anderson children, you too are getting older and beginning to lose the fearlessness of a young child. Pray for boldness. Only the devil wants you to be afraid of being made fun of for talking about Jesus. Remember what a life-saving message the gospel of Jesus is. When you speak of Jesus' suffering and death on the cross to someone who does not believe, you are actually helping to pull that person away from an eternity of torment in hell.

As the years go by, keep in mind the confidence you once had. When it comes to sharing the message of Jesus with someone else, may we all be filled with a child's fearlessness.

Prayer: Dear Jesus, give me a stronger faith so I may talk about you boldly to my friends and those I meet. Remind me that your word is always full of power and will have an effect on those who hear it. Amen.

Ice Palace

Keep your lives free from the love of money and be content with what you have, because God has said, "Never will I leave you; never will I forsake you." (Hebrews 13:5)

"It's not fair!" Melissa Anderson cried, as she flounced onto her bed. Her bottom lip stuck out in a discouraged little pout.

"Have you been outside?" asked her sister Lindsay, looking up from her homework. "Your bottom lip is frozen in a mighty strange position."

Melissa shot her sister an irritated glance. "I'm in no mood for your jokes. I'm mad. Dad won't let me go skating at the Ice Palace on Saturday. He says it costs too much."

"It does!" Lindsay answered. "Besides, weren't you there just two weekends ago? What's wrong with the skating rink in the park? I used to skate there all the time when I was your age."

"Nobody goes to the park any more," Melissa sputtered. "It's so . . . so . . . so unsophisticated."

"Yes, but it doesn't cost anything either," Lindsay reminded her.

Melissa's lip began to bulge out again. "I still don't think it's fair!" she squawked as she began to page through a teen magazine. A picture of one of the flashy teen movie stars suddenly caught her eye. She held it up for Lindsay to see. "If I were a movie star, money wouldn't stop me from doing what I wanted."

Lindsay sighed as she picked up her geography book and walked over to Melissa's bed. "We're studying the country of Africa this month." She opened the book and pointed to a picture of starving Ethiopian children.

"Oooh!" Melissa cried in disgust. "What's the matter with that baby's stomach? And, look, his legs are so skinny, but his stomach is fat."

"It's called malnutrition. Lots of kids over in Africa don't get enough to eat and are dying from malnutrition."

Melissa swallowed hard. The picture had struck home. "This poor fella will probably never know what the Ice Palace is!" she replied sadly.

"Probably not!" Lindsay replied. "I'm sure that right now he'd settle for the leftovers we often leave on our plates after supper."

Melissa was silent for a long time as she flipped through the pages of Lindsay's geography book. "This little African boy probably envies me as much as I envied that movie star. To him, I must seem to have everything."

"You do," Lindsay replied. "We both do. Sometimes I forget that, too. I mean, we are part of a Christian family, we have a wonderful home and more than enough food on our plates. We even get to go out to eat once in a while.

"And go to the Ice Palace," Melissa added.

"Come to think about it, we have it even better than this movie star!" Lindsay said. "We've been brought to faith in Jesus our Savior. All the money in the world couldn't buy heaven for us."

"I was so angry when Dad told me I couldn't go to the Ice Palace," Melissa confessed. "Now I feel really guilty. Before I came up here, I glanced at our church envelope sitting on the dining room hutch. Dad had already made out the check. I was so upset because the price of a ticket to the Ice Palace was so small when compared to the amount Dad gives to church. I figured I could have used some of that."

Lindsay nodded. "Dad and Mom know that God expects those whom he has blessed with so much, to give more of what they have to those in need."

Melissa rose from her bed, suddenly filled with enthusiasm. "Tomorrow our Sunday School offering will be sent to Peru. I'm going to include an extra gift in my envelope. Maybe it's time I show my thankfulness for all the blessings God has given me.

"And what about the Ice Palace?" asked Lindsay.

"Oh, someone told me the ice on the park's skating rink was just as good!" she grinned. "Anyway, a person should be satisfied with her blessings instead of always wanting more!"

"Especially when those blessings include Jesus our Savior," Lindsay answered. "It's sure nice to see your lip back where it belongs, Melissa!"

Prayer: Dear Jesus, I am sorry I am not always satisfied with the blessings you have given me. Help me to want to use my money to bring others to faith in you as well as to show my thankfulness to you for loving me so. Amen.

Adding Or Subtracting From God's Word?

But let the one who has my word speak it faithfully.
(Jeremiah 23:28)

The Anderson twins rushed through the doorway, bursting with excitement. "You'll never guess what we saw on the way home from school, Mom," Melissa began. "There was a terrible car accident at the corner of 5th and Menlo."

"It was a five-car pile-up!" Michael chattered on.

"A three-car pile-up," Melissa corrected her brother. "One of the cars hit a fire hydrant and water was spraying all over the street."

"Practically the whole fire department was sitting in the intersection trying to stop the water," Michael added.

"Not the whole department, Michael," Melissa interrupted him. "But, I did see one fire truck."

"Yeah, and one car was tipped over on its top! A little baby and his mom were trapped inside."

"Well, the car was almost on its top," Melissa answered. "It was on its side, and the boy was about five years old."

"And all the blood! It was over everything! So many were hurt!" exclaimed Michael.

"Well, the blood wasn't over everything," Melissa explained. "The water was everywhere. But I did see one man holding his head and another was limping into a police car."

Mrs. Anderson stopped peeling the vegetables for supper and fixed both eyes on her children. "Are you two sure you saw the same accident?" Mom asked. "You both are describing it very differently."

"Well, Mom, I had to spice it up a little bit so you'd know how terrible it was!" exclaimed Michael.

"Yeah," chuckled Melissa, "my way is really what happened. Michael's is the TV version."

We all know what Melissa meant by the TV version. Everything portrayed on TV is bigger, bolder, more exciting, and more colorful. TV likes to dramatize everything to attract our attention.

We've all seen TV's version of certain Bible stories. TV likes to pep up the stories by adding to them, trying to make them more exciting. On the other hand, important bits of information are very often left out to make the story more acceptable to those who don't believe the Bible is the true Word of God.

God, however, is very clear when it comes to those who want to change his word. He wants nothing to be left out or added to it. For example, when we talk about Jesus as a good teacher, let us never leave out the important fact that he is also true God and our Savior. Or when we tell how Jesus suffered and died on the cross, we also will want to include the miracle of his resurrection. We have to make it known that our Jesus is not a dead Savior, but a living one.

God's word has power in and of itself. It doesn't need us to add to it or subtract from it to make it better. It is holy and perfect already. It is strong enough to make a sinner sorry for his sin and gentle enough to lead him to Jesus his Savior. Do you understand now why it is so important to read and study God's word? When you know what it says, the stronger your faith will become and the better you will be able to tell others about its saving good news.

Prayer: Dear Jesus, forgive me if I have ever added or taken away from the truth your word teaches. I want to keep it as pure as you gave it to me. Amen.

It Hurts

And we know that in all things God works for the good of those who love him, who have been called according to his purpose. (Romans 8:28)

Mom hung up the phone and stared blankly at Dad. "Lindsay was calling from the emergency room. The ambulance just rushed little Jeffie Maas to the hospital. His hand and forearm are badly burned."

By the time Lindsay's parents arrived at the hospital, little Jeffie's hand was bandaged. He sat on Lindsay's lap, clinging tightly to his baby-sitter. Tears streamed down Lindsay's cheeks as she spilled out the entire story.

"I had to run upstairs for just a second. Baby Caroline had just awakened from her nap. I was lifting her out of her crib when I heard Jeffie scream. When I raced downstairs, Jeffie was sitting on the counter next to the stove top, and all four stove burners were red hot. The doctor says he has second and first degree burns on his arm and hand."

"Hot! Hot!" Jeffie emphasized the terrible discovery he had made.

Later, after they were back home and Jeffie's parents had come for him, Mom, Dad, and Lindsay sat in the kitchen with a comforting cup of hot tea. "I don't think I can bear anything hot right now!" Lindsay exclaimed, pushing the drink away.

"This is all my fault. Now little Jeffie will have to suffer weeks of pain. Why does God let little children feel such pain?"

"We wish we could feel the pain for them," Mom agreed, "but it may surprise you, Lindsay, that pain isn't really all bad. Pain is never easy to take because it does hurt, but could you imagine what would have happened if Jeffie hadn't felt the pain and pulled his hand away from the hot stove?"

Lindsay covered her mouth. "His hand may have been burned beyond repair!"

Dad nodded. "In fact, Jeffie's ability to feel pain may have saved his life. Dr. Franke noticed a long pink streak on the back of Jeffie's leg. He thinks Jeffie may have been sitting on top of one of the burners. He apparently began to move off when it became too uncomfortable to stay there."

"Jeffie's clothing and hair could have caught on fire if he hadn't felt the pain!" Lindsay said, looking horrified. "I never thought I'd ever be thankful for pain."

Have you ever wanted to do away with pain? It may surprise you when people talk about pain as something good. We all know what pain feels like. It isn't fun, and worst of all "it hurts!"

Jesus, our Savior, knows all about pain, too. If we had stood at the foot of the cross and watched when he suffered and died, we might have thought that the pain he was going through was anything but good. He was suffering in agony. It was as terrible as living through eternity in hell itself.

But no matter how terrible the thorns, the beatings, the nails, and mocking were for Jesus, we must realize they were a good kind of pain for us! When he was made to endure so much misery, Jesus wasn't being taught a lesson as Jeffie was. Jesus is holy. He knew and kept God's commandments perfectly, and he did it all in our place. His pain on the cross was for our good, because all his suffering washed away our sins and the punishment we deserved for them.

Jesus felt pain in his heart as well as his body. He was

friendless, mocked, and made to be the worst criminal there ever was, because our sins were put upon him. Since Jesus, the holy Son of God, felt this horrible pain in his body and soul, he knows how much we hurt when we feel pain. And because Jesus faced this pain with courage, for us, some day all pain will be wiped away forever in heaven!

Prayer: Dear Jesus, help me to bear all the pains of this life. Thank you for bearing the worst pain of all on the cross so that my sins could be forgiven. Amen.

I Will Never Leave You

I will never leave you nor forsake you. (Joshua 1:5)

"Please, Melissa, don't read another word," Tracy sobbed.

Melissa looked down at her little sister in bewilderment. "But, Tracy, you usually love the story of *Walter The Lazy Mouse.*"

"I used to," Tracy replied glumly, "up until this morning. Remember? I didn't get up right away, and no one was upstairs to help me get the toothpaste out of the tube or to help me get my socks out of the top drawer. Dad called everyone to breakfast, and I was still missing one shoe. I felt just as miserable as poor Walter in the story."

Melissa smiled and patted her younger sister's shoulder. "Tracy, in the story, Walter was really slow and *lazy*. It took him days just to walk home from school," she chuckled.

"Yeah, and one day it took so long for him to come home that his parents forgot all about him and moved away! I could just see that happening to me because sometimes I'm just as slow."

"Oh, Tracy," Melissa hugged her sister. "The story of Walter is just make-believe. You are a little slower at getting ready because you are little. Mom and Dad would never leave you just because you were a few minutes late getting down to breakfast."

Have you ever felt like five-year-old Tracy? Sometimes we wonder if anyone really likes us and cares about us. Will my friends always stick by me? Will Mom and Dad still love me even if I'm bad? Like Tracy, we may even no longer want to hear favorite stories—even if they are funny—if they remind us of something that's not very pleasant for us, like being deserted.

Just as Melissa put a comforting arm around her sister, God wants to comfort us. The same promise he made to Joshua long ago he holds out to us. God says, "I will not leave you nor forsake you" (Joshua 1:15).

God's promise is sure. We can depend upon it. Friends and relatives sometimes let us down, and they may even go away and leave us, but God never will. In Isaiah 49:16 God tells us, "See, I have engraved you on the palms of my hands." Is it possible to rub a tattoo off? That is how impossible it is for God to rub you out of his hands.

Those "love marks" on Jesus' hands and feet were not easily acquired. He suffered six agonizing hours of pain as the nails of the cross ripped into his hands and feet. This proof of his love for us, as well as his promise always to forgive our sins, is never-ending. These marks of love are, indeed, a blessed assurance that Jesus will never forsake us.

Jesus knows how it feels to be lonely and friendless, to have friends turn their backs on us when we need them the most. Jesus' friends ran away when the soldiers arrested him. On the cross, Jesus even felt the torture of being forsaken by God. Remember the words he spoke in agony? "My God, my God, why have you forsaken me?" (Mark 15:34). Jesus bore the sins of the whole world on the cross and was forsaken there by his very own Father. Jesus became sin for us, so that we'd never be forsaken as he was.

What comfort this is for all of us. The one whose company

really counts will never leave us. Jesus was alone, despised, and forsaken even unto death, that we might have peace, love, joy, and eternal life in him.

Prayer: Dear Jesus, remind us when we are lonely and feel left out, how lonely and despised you became for us. Forgive us our many sins that they may never make us strangers from you. Amen.

Honesty, Even To The Last Penny

He who has been stealing must steal no longer, but must work, doing something useful with his own hands, that he may have something to share with those in need. (Ephesians 4:28)

As Lindsay opened the front door, Jason trumpeted loudly, "*Crispy Chicken*, home of the crispiest, tastiest, most 'mouth-wateringest' chicken in the world."

"Please, Jason," Lindsay groaned, "not the *Crispy Chicken* theme song tonight! *Crispy Chicken* just fired Jill Stanley."

"How can a chicken fire anyone?" Michael asked with a smirk.

Lindsay tried not to smile. "She was really fired by Mr. Potz, our boss. She flunked his honesty test."

"What is Mr. Potz' honesty test?" asked Melissa.

"Oh, he leaves money lying around the restaurant to see if his workers will pocket it or return it to his office."

"When you were hired, did Mr. Potz tell you to return any lost money to him?" Mom asked.

"Well, yes, but we didn't know he was trying to trap us, and we certainly didn't think any of us would lose our jobs over it."

"It does sound like a strict policy, but Mr. Potz has every right to demand honest employees," Dad said.

"Jill understands that perfectly, but Mr. Potz fired her for keeping 65 cents in small change, not a ten or twenty-dollar bill!"

"The amount isn't the issue with Mr. Potz. He simply wants employees he can trust with any amount, whether it's pennies or a register bursting with cash," Mom reminded Lindsay.

Lindsay nodded and sighed, "Jill lost so much for so little."

"Well, Lindsay, remember how in the Bible one dishonest move also caused Elisha's servant Gehazi to lose so much," Dad answered.

"Oh, I remember that story," Michael nodded. "Elisha, the prophet, had just healed Naaman of his leprosy. Naaman wanted to pay Elisha, but he refused. Elisha wanted God to have all the glory."

Mom nodded. "After Naaman left, greedy Gehazi ran after him and said Elisha had changed his mind. Two young men had just arrived at the prophet's home. Now Elisha really needed money and clothes for these two men."

"What a greedy, terrible lie!" Jason answered. "God punished Gehazi right away by giving him Naaman's leprosy."

Lindsay shuddered. "Money and clothes in exchange for leprosy!"

"Wasn't God being a little hard on Gehazi?" asked Melissa.

"We must never question God's actions," Dad explained. "For one thing, this harsh punishment makes us realize, too, just what our sins really deserve. It's so easy to forget that. And remember, God was leading Gehazi to repent of his sin. He was trying to draw him closer to himself."

"Do you think God is doing the same thing for Jill?" Lindsay asked.

Mom nodded. "Hopefully, Jill will feel sorry she took the money, no matter how small the amount was. And certainly for the rest of her life she'll remember how important it is to be honest even in small things."

"Jill said she was sorry. She just doesn't think she'll ever be able to get over being fired," Lindsay answered.

"Then you'll want to comfort her," Mom answered. "Remind her that Jesus has forgiven all of our sins. Since we believe and trust in his forgiveness, it is time to put both her sin and its punishment behind her. If Jill becomes a trustworthy person from this experience, it was worth the cost of her job at Crispy Chicken."

"Even if it *is* the crispiest, tastiest, most 'mouthwateringest' chicken in the world!" Jason chuckled.

Prayer: Dear Jesus, please forgive my greedy, dishonest heart. Help me to confess all my sins before you. Help me to understand any discipline that you send is your way of drawing me closer to you. Amen.

Just Yes Or No

Simply let your "Yes" be "Yes," and your "No," "No"; anything beyond this comes from the evil one. (Matthew 5:37)

Tracy Anderson came running into the kitchen. Her face was steamy and red from playing outside. "Mom, Mom!" she called. "Melissa swore! I heard her!"

Mrs. Anderson scooped her five-year-old daughter into her lap and listened as she explained what had happened. "Mary wouldn't believe Melissa jumped three hundred times without a miss!"

Mrs. Anderson heard a slight rustling noise at the back door. With a quiet cough, Melissa reluctantly entered the kitchen. "I had no choice, Mom. I had to swear to get Mary to believe me."

"Does she believe you now?" Mom asked.

"I don't know," Melissa shrugged. "She still wants to see me do it."

"Oh, I think she believes you," Tracy argued. "You did swear to kiss Bobby Freemont if you were lying."

Melissa blushed with shame and listened with her head bowed as her mother spoke. "God doesn't want his children to swear about foolish things. Suppose you had miscounted and didn't jump exactly 300 times? Would you really go kiss Bobby to keep your oath?"

"Oh, Mom, Mary wouldn't really expect me to kiss him. It was just something I said so she'd believe me."

"Many other people think swearing by God's name isn't serious either, but it is, Melissa. Did you know you were actually calling on God as your witness that you were telling the truth, and that you were asking God to punish you if you weren't telling the truth?"

"Do you mean I'm asking God to punish me if I'm lying?" gulped Melissa.

Mom nodded solemnly as Melissa's twin brother appeared in the doorway. "Swearing foolishly can get you into a lot of trouble!" Michael said. "Remember the story of King Herod?"

Melissa nodded. "He swore he'd give Herodias's daughter anything she wanted, up to half his kingdom if she'd dance for him."

"Little did he know she'd ask for the head of John the Baptist on a silver platter!" Michael replied.

Tracy winced. "Did he really have John killed?"

Mrs. Anderson nodded sadly. "He didn't want to lose face in front of his guests. He committed the sin of murder to keep his sinful oath."

Melissa listened anxiously. Tiny drops of sweat popped out on her forehead. "Are you still worried about your oath?" Mom asked in a kind voice.

"I think I jumped 300 times, but I *could* have counted wrong!"

"Should Melissa go over and give Bobby a kiss, just to be on the safe side?" Michael giggled.

Mom frowned at her young son. "I think a prayer of sincere sorrow would be even better," Mom answered. "And, remember, the next time a simple 'yes' or 'no' will be more pleasing to God than a foolish oath."

"How precious do you hold God's name? To some, the name of God is a big joke. Many people don't believe God exists. However, we who have been brought to faith, believe it was God's Son Jesus who paid for our sins on the cross. There is no name more precious or sweeter in our language. May we all guard our lips to speak God's name, only to his glory and not to our shame."

Prayer: Dear Jesus, forgive me when I use your name in a careless or sinful way. Help me to guard my lips so that I use your name only for your glory and that I may never use it to my shame. Amen.

Happy With What I Am

This is the day the LORD has made; let us rejoice and be glad in it. (Psalm 118:24)

Jason pushed the back door open roughly. He yanked at the refrigerator handle, pulled out the ice tray, and dumped two ice cubes into his glass. Lindsay looked up from the sewing machine. "Basketball tryouts didn't go very well?" she asked gently.

"I don't get to play on the eighth grade team; I have to play first string seventh grade." Jason spit out the words.

"Don't forget, Jay, you are in seventh grade," Lindsay reminded him. "There's no shame in having to play on the same team with your classmates."

Jason slumped into a chair beside his sister. "But Coach told me I was good enough for Varsity."

Lindsay stopped the machine suddenly. "Oh, I almost forgot. You got a letter from our cousin Jeremy today."

"Jeremy?" Jason's mouth went dry. Jeremy was his age, but three years ago he had broken his back in a diving accident. The injury had left him paralyzed from the neck down. "But how can Jeremy write? He can't move his hands."

"He writes with his teeth, Jason. He's been learning ever since the accident. He says this little note took him almost one whole week to write."

As Jason scanned the three short sentences and gazed at the picture of his cousin taped to the back of the letter, his anger was replaced with shame. He looked down at his two strong arms and his two strong legs. "I'm glad Jeremy wasn't here to see me carrying on," Jason admitted. "He'd give anything just to play a good game of one-on-one like we used to."

"He'd give anything just to be able to walk across the floor and help himself to his own ice water like you just did," Lindsay corrected him.

"Jeremy is the one who really has the right to complain!" Jason added.

"No," Lindsay persisted. "No one has that right, not even a paraplegic."

"Now, who has the unfeeling heart?" Jason asked. "How would you like to be trapped in a wheelchair for the rest of your life?"

Lindsay shuddered. "It would be terribly difficult if that happened, but complaining would only make me bitter and a bear to live with."

"How do you suppose Jeremy keeps the smile on his face?" Jason asked, showing his sister the picture.

"Mom says he reads his Bible constantly. He especially loves the passages which remind him that God hasn't forgotten him. Then there's Martin, Jeremy's paraplegic friend. He's convinced Jeremy that life can be worth living again, even from a wheelchair. Martin says that Jeremy can even be better than he was before."

"Better? Even without the use of his arms and legs?" asked Jason. "How could that be?"

"Well, as a paraplegic he can be more understanding about others in the same condition. Because he knows what they are going through, he may find it easier to talk to them about how Jesus gave up his life for them on the cross."

"I wonder if God is turning Jeremy's terrible accident into a blessing for other paraplegics."

Lindsay nodded. "God does use our troubles and our failures to make us humble and bring us closer to him. You could look at not making the first string varsity basketball team as one of those times."

Jason smiled and nodded. He scanned his cousin's penmanship again. "Imagine the patience it took to write a whole page with just teeth!"

Lindsay nodded. "Instead of complaining, Jeremy is using all that energy to praise God!"

Prayer: Dear Jesus, I am sorry I complain so often. Help me to count my blessings instead of finding fault with the way you have made me. Help me use the tragedies in my life to bring others closer to you as their Savior. Amen.

When I Am Weak, That's When I'm Strong

That is why, for Christ's sake, I delight in weaknesses, in insults, in hardships, in persecutions, in difficulties. For when I am weak, then I am strong. **(2 Corinthians 12:10)**

Lindsay was seated in front of the mirror, combing her long hair. Her upper lip trembled and a single tear slid down her cheek. She carefully placed her glasses on the dresser top, and her head sunk unto her arm.

"What's wrong?" asked Mrs. Anderson who had just entered the girls' room to put the freshly washed clothing away. She wrapped a consoling arm around her daughter and lifted her chin.

"It's these stupid glasses," sobbed Lindsay. "I wish I wouldn't have to wear them."

"But I thought you liked the new frames we picked out," Mom answered. "You said yourself that it is wonderful to have clear eyesight."

"It is wonderful. Everything isn't so blurry any more. But why can't I see without glasses like other kids do? They are such a bother! I have to wear a strap to hold them on during basketball practice. Next quarter we have swimming in P.E. I'll be my old blind self again under the water." Lindsay moaned.

Mom nodded knowingly. "I had to get glasses too when I was about your age. It took me a long time to get used to my 'new' face. I never thought a boy would look at me again because of my glasses."

"What did you do?" asked Lindsay.

"At first I stopped wearing them at school, but that didn't work. After seeing the world clearly for once, I couldn't bear to go back to a blur again. Finally, I decided to pray about it. I knew God had the power to heal my nearsightedness. For three years I prayed for good eyesight."

"What made you stop praying?" asked Lindsay. "Was it because God didn't give you what you asked for?"

"No," Mom answered, "in fact, I could still be praying about it. But I felt God was teaching me something more important by making me wear glasses. I realized that even though my eyes weren't perfect, God still had given me what I needed to be happy."

Lindsay nodded. "By 'what I needed to be happy' do you mean the gift of a Savior in Jesus?"

"Exactly! Jesus' love for me was enough. He had already given me the most important thing—the forgiveness of sins. Jesus had accepted me just as I was, and I realized I could, too. You could say that wearing glasses forced me to look to Jesus for my strength and assurance, instead of myself."

It was no accident that Mrs. Anderson felt this way. When she was young, she had been reading about the apostle Paul in her Bible. Paul also had some bodily weakness he wished God would heal. After praying three times for this "thorn in the flesh"—as he called it—to go away, God told Paul his *grace* was enough for him. Paul's weakness made him rely on Christ, instead of on his own power and ability. Depending upon Christ for everything made Paul really strong!

You may be discouraged about some weakness you were born with. You may have poor hearing, poor eyesight, a weak heart, or asthma. Some day you may be cured, or God may decide it is better for you to live with your ailment. However it turns out for you, God wants you to cling to him for help through all your troubles. Because, even in our weaknesses, we can be strong in Jesus our Savior!

Prayer: Dear Jesus, please help me to keep praying to you in every need. Help me to accept myself as I am. Thank you for giving me forgiveness from my sins. You have made me truly strong in you. Amen.

First, You've Got To Hear The Bad News

So the law was put in charge to lead us to Christ that we might be justified by faith. (Galatians 3:24)

Jason Anderson held the pine board tightly as his dad hammered together the simple frame for Tracy's small book shelf. Mr. Anderson stopped his work as soon as he noticed the deep creases in his son's forehead.

"You'll bore a hole right through this new wood if you think any harder," Dad kidded him.

Jason chuckled. "I was thinking about the boy who lives down the street. His name is Jimmy and we're on the same baseball team. I tried telling him about Jesus today during practice. He could have cared less. He acts like he doesn't need a Savior at all!"

Mr. Anderson held three nails in his mouth as he thought for a moment. After hammering the second shelf into place, he spoke. "Maybe you're coming with the good news before Jimmy has heard the bad!"

"What do you mean?" asked Jason.

"Remember our vacation out west two summers ago?"

"Sure," replied Jason. "We visited Uncle George in the Arizona desert. He's got to live in the hottest place in the whole world!"

"Yes, at 120 degrees in the shade it was terribly hot," Dad laughed. "Remember the new house they were building next to Uncle George's?"

Jason nodded. "We were able to see the foundation poured and the whole wooden frame nailed together."

"On the first day of their work," Dad continued, "did the workers bring their big shovel and just start digging?"

"Oh, no," replied Jason. "Don't you remember, Dad? Uncle George told us they would damage their shovels if they did that. The ground was too hard to dig through."

Dad nodded. "Right! So they let the water sprinklers run for two whole days to soften the hard ground. Well, in a way, you might say Jimmy's heart is like that hard, stony ground."

"Oh, I see," Jason answered as he caught on to what Dad was trying to tell him. "When I tell Jimmy how much he needs Jesus, it doesn't sink in because he's not ready for it."

"Exactly!" Dad answered. "Jimmy needs his heart softened. He has to know why he needs Jesus so much. He has to know what a terrible sinner he is before he sees any real need for a Savior. So you have to teach him the law first. That also is a very important part of God's word."

"But, Dad," Jason complained, "we learned in school that the law is the Ten Commandments. No one can keep those."

Dad nodded. "Exactly. This is the law's purpose. When Jimmy realizes he can't keep the law perfectly, think how helpless he'll feel. He'll realize he deserves punishment, and there's nothing in his own power he can do to change it. Just like water made the hard ground ready for a shovel, Jimmy's heart will be ready to hear the good news about Jesus."

Jason nodded and smiled. "It was never much fun telling Jimmy about Jesus before. It was like talking to a brick wall. Now, it'll be like throwing him a life preserver."

Dad nodded. "And let's pray he will cling to this good news with all his heart as we Christians do."

Prayer: Dear Jesus, remind me of my sin. I would die in hell without you, my Savior. Please forgive all my wrong doing, and take me with you to your home in heaven. Amen.

Obeying All The Time

Obey your leaders and submit to their authority. They keep watch over you as men who must give an account. (Hebrews 13:17)

"Tracy!" Mom called, "Come and set the table."

Obediently, Tracy laid her dolls aside, washed her hands, and began to place the plates on the table. As she set out the silverware, cups, and napkins, Tracy did not even lift her eyes to meet her mother's gaze. She was angry, and she didn't care whether it showed or not.

Mom noticed. She gently took her daughter's hand and led her to the kitchen chair. Lifting her tiny chin, she asked, "Are you still angry with me for punishing you for going over to Eric's house without asking?"

Tracy nodded. "It was the first time I did it. Couldn't you have given me another chance? Why do I have to obey all the time?"

"Once there was a little girl just about your age who wondered the very same thing," Mom replied. "She knew it was important to obey her parents. She tried her best to keep all the rules at home and in school. Well, one day she was walking home from school. It was such a long way home, and the little girl's feet were so very tired. A really nice looking man drove up and asked this little girl if she could use a ride."

Tracy sat bolt-upright. "Did she go with the stranger?" she asked anxiously. "You know, nice looking people don't always turn out to be so nice."

"This little girl was thinking the very same thing. She remembered her parents warning her never to ride with strangers, but she had so far to walk, and her new shoes were pinching her feet terribly. She thought it wouldn't hurt to disobey just this once."

"Oh, no," Tracy answered, "just disobeying once could have cost her life. What if the man wouldn't take her home? Did she get into his car?"

"She opened the door, got halfway in, and then she felt someone tug her shoulder very hard. She fell backwards on the cement."

"Who kept her from getting in?" asked Melissa.

"My brother," Mom replied. "He scolded me all the way home, and when we got there, he told my mother and father what I had done."

"You were the little girl?" Tracy asked in surprise.

Mom nodded. "From that day on, I learned a very important lesson about obeying. Just disobeying *once* could have meant my life."

"Is that the reason you punished me for going over to Eric's without permission?"

Mom nodded. "Learning to obey parents' rules all the time will help you learn to obey God's rules all the time. God's rules are the Ten Commandments. They tell us what to do and what not to do. They tell us we shouldn't steal or lie or hate anyone."

"But how can I be good all the time?" asked Tracy.

"You can't. None of us can, because we are sinful. But a person who trusts in Jesus as his Savior will feel sorry when he sins. He'll quickly say he is sorry and ask for forgiveness. He won't whine and ask, 'Why do I have to obey all the time?' "

Tracy blushed and smiled. "A person who loves Jesus will be happy to obey all the time. After all, Jesus didn't grumble when he died for my sins on the cross. He was glad to suffer in my place."

"He didn't enjoy the pain," Mom answered, "but because he loved us so much, he wanted to give us eternal life in heaven. Yet, we could only have heaven if our sins were forgiven. So he took all of our sins upon himself and made sure they were all washed away."

Tracy smiled and jumped off the kitchen chair. "Next time I'll be sure to ask before going over to Eric's." She touched her mother's forehead to her own. "Will you promise never to get into a stranger's car?"

"Your Uncle Stuart made sure I learned that lesson long, long ago!"

Prayer: Dear Jesus, sometimes I feel stubborn inside, not wanting to obey all the time. Please forgive my stubborn feelings. Help me to obey those you have placed over me. I want to thank them for watching over me, body and soul. Amen.

Room For One More

But when the time had fully come, God sent his Son, born of a woman, born under law, to redeem those under law, that we might receive the full rights of sons. (Galatians 4:4,5)

Jason Anderson ducked his head into the bathroom where Lindsay was brushing her teeth. "Have you heard the latest?" he whispered. "Mom and Dad plan to adopt little Justin."

Lindsay's arm froze in mid-air. "Who told you that?" she whispered in alarm. "Keeping Justin here after his parents' car accident was not supposed to be permanent. I distinctly heard Aunt Mary tell Mom at the funeral that she planned to adopt Justin."

"It looks as though her plans fell through," Jason shrugged.

Lindsay sighed heavily. "I do love the little guy, but before long he'll be into my things just like Tracy used to be."

"What about us boys?" Jason asked. "We have to sleep in the same room with him. His baby clothes and diapers take up an awful lot of space."

Melissa and I will be stuck baby-sitting all the time. Poor Tracy will lose her place as the youngest in the family," Lindsay pouted.

"Then it's up to us to vote Justin out," Jason decided. "It's not fair of Mom and Dad to ask us to add another brother to the family. Don't we count?"

That evening, after little Justin was put to bed, the Anderson children trooped down the stairs to speak to Mom and Dad. Lindsay and Jason had been elected to tell Mom and Dad how the rest of the kids felt. While they talked, the others nodded their agreement. When Lindsay and Jason finished, the five children stood quietly awaiting the verdict.

Dad coughed and cleared his throat. "If you all feel so strongly against making Justin a permanent member of the family, I will ask one of Justin's uncles to adopt him. Would all of you agree to Uncle George taking him?"

The Anderson children nodded and smiled eagerly. "Although, if Uncle George takes him, little Justin will probably never see the inside of a church building again," Dad informed them.

Lindsay twisted uncomfortably. "I didn't think about that," she admitted. "There will be no one to take Justin to Sunday School either as he gets older."

"Or make sure he hears a Bible story for his little devotions at night," Tracy added sadly.

"It almost seems as though it is up to us whether or not Justin is raised in a place where his faith has a chance to stay strong or shrivel and die," Jason added thoughtfully.

"Somehow having more space in my room doesn't seem quite as important now," Michael admitted.

And who wants to be the baby of the family forever?" grinned Tracy.

"Dad?" Melissa asked. "If it's all right with you and Mom, we'd like to change our vote. Could little Justin be a keeper?"

A long time ago all of us were in the same situation as little Justin, but in a spiritual way. The Jews were God's chosen people. As Gentiles we had no right to call God our Father, but God also wanted us in his family, even though we were strangers. As a branch of an orange tree can be grafted into the trunk of a grapefruit tree, God grafted us into his family. All those who trust and love him are part of God's family and are called God's children. Like little Justin, we were adopted into God's family. We are forever "God's keepers."

Prayer: Dear Father, thank you for adopting me as your child through baptism. Give me the courage to talk to others about your son Jesus, my Savior. Let them believe in Jesus' forgiveness and love him as I do. Amen.

True Wisdom

But grow in the grace and knowledge of our Lord and Savior Jesus Christ. To him be glory both now and forever! Amen. (2 Peter 3:18)

"What are you reading?" asked Melissa, as she walked into her twin brother's bedroom.

"It's a book called *Fun Facts*," Michael answered. "It's filled with all kinds of interesting information. Here's a fact you've never heard, I'll bet. Did you know spiders can go 17 months without food, and snakes can fast for a two-year stretch?"

"Really?" Melissa laughed. "Here, let me read one," she begged as she reached for the book. "It says here someone timed a snail and found it took the little guy 14 days to travel one mile." Melissa smiled. "I wonder who wasted two weeks discovering that bit of information!"

Michael shrugged and pulled the book back. "It was probably the same guy who found out this snail could crawl over the sharpest razor without cutting himself."

Melissa continued to read over her brother's shoulder. "Or the same fellow who discovered a whale's right nostril is always larger than its left," she laughed.

The Anderson twins chuckled through the numerous pages of Michael's *Fun Facts*. It was cleverly written and quite entertaining, even to the point of sparking the children's interest in the study of certain plants and animals.

The whole world is filled with knowledge. God created it bursting with unanswered questions. He wants us to keep our minds active as we discover all the complicated facts about his beautiful earth. Unfortunately, many people are interested *only* in this kind of information. They are more curious about studying the unique habits of toads and snails than they are about digging into the pages of God's Word.

A young person may be able to discuss the subjects of math, science, and history quite intelligently. But if he doesn't understand he is a sinner in urgent need of a Savior, all his learning is really worthless. Only the Bible reveals how Jesus suffered on the cross for our sin. Only through the word of God does the Holy Spirit work faith in our hearts so that we believe Jesus truly rose from the dead and won the battle for us against sin, death, and hell.

As you grow older, you will find the world is filled with people who scoff at the Bible's teachings. They may say that the Bible is unscientific. They may say that many of the stories in the Bible are only fables and myths. Don't be swayed by their way of thinking. Even though some of these people may know a great deal about stars, toads, and snails, they don't have God's gift of spiritual wisdom as you do.

The Holy Spirit is now working in you. To you the Bible is far from foolish. It is God's plan of salvation. You need only to realize that you must keep studying it over and over again for your faith to remain strong and sure.

As a young person, you have more time for reading and study than you will probably have at any other time of your life. Search and discover all you can about God's beautiful universe. Hold your Bible and the study of it higher than any of your other books. It is the only book which is able to show you the way to heaven and to make you truly wise.

Prayer: Dear Jesus, help me to remember that you alone have the words for eternal life—words which are recorded in the Bible. Help me to study your Word more, so I may be truly wise in what really matters. Amen.

One Sin

Therefore, just as sin entered the world through one man, and death through sin, and in this way death came to all men, because all sinned. (Romans 5:12)

Lindsay and Melissa cleared the table and stacked the dishes neatly on the counter near the sink. "Hand me that empty milk carton," Lindsay instructed her younger sister. I'll pour this warm grease into it before it cools and hardens. Then it'll be ready for the waste basket."

"Why fuss over a little cup of grease?" asked Melissa. "It looks just like water to me. Pour it down the sink."

Lindsay shook her head and reached for the carton herself. "It may look clear like water, but Dad says that as it thickens, it becomes like cement and will clog the pipes."

Melissa shrugged. "It's only a little bit. A little bit wouldn't hurt. Who would know?"

A little grease down the drain, who would know? Taking candy from the store without paying, who would know? In and of themselves a tiny drop of grease down a drain, or a tiny lie to our parents seems so small. What is the real harm?

Melissa's tiny cupful of grease can turn into a giant-sized clog only the Roto-Rooter man can loosen. The tiniest of sins—the rude remark or a small bit of gossip—comes from an attitude of the heart which says to God, "I don't care about what you want. I'll do just as I please."

Just as the Roto-Rooter man uses a metal coil to break through the clog, God uses his law to break down our proud attitudes. He uses troubles, our parents' discipline, and life's griefs to make us realize how much we need a Savior.

If Melissa had poured the cup of grease down the sink, only she, and eventually the Roto-Rooter man, would know about it. There are also some sins we commit which only we and God know about. If a cupful of grease is serious to a Roto-Rooter man, think how much more serious every sin is to God—yes, including those which build up and eventually "plug" our hearts.

When you sin, don't hide it. Don't cover it up. Repent of it. Ask God's forgiveness. Even the worst of your sins has been paid for by the blood of God's Son, Jesus. His death on the cross has made our hearts clean, unclogged from sin and right with God.

A tiny bit of grease down the sink, what's the harm? The person who must clear the drain in your house would cringe at such words. One sin—a single thought—what's so bad about that? May this attitude make us cringe and quickly lead us to seek the forgiveness of our Lord who gave his life for all our sins.

Prayer: Dear Jesus, remind me how serious my sins are. Help me to be totally disgusted when I see sin, especially in myself. Forgive all my sins for your sake. Amen.

God's Whipping Boy

But he was pierced for our transgressions, he was crushed for our iniquities; the punishment that brought us peace was upon him, and by his wounds we are healed. **(Isaiah 53:5)**

Jason sat in the porch swing sprawled full length across the wooden slats, completely absorbed in a book. Michael busily rolled his toy cars in and out of his brother's dangling legs. The title of Jason's book, *The Whipping Boy*, suddenly caught his eye. Michael asked, "What is a whipping boy?"

"It's a boy who gets whipped," Jason answered casually, not moving his eyes from the page.

"But why does the boy get whipped?" Michael persisted.

Jason sighed and laid the book in his lap. "He gets whipped for the bad things other people do."

"I've never heard of anything so unfair!" Michael protested.

"Neither have I," Jason agreed, "but around the 16th century when kings and queens ruled many lands, whipping boys were quite common. Apparently some of the people figured that since the prince or princess would grow up and rule the country some day, it wasn't smart to go around spanking them. So a whipping boy was punished instead for the bad things the prince or princess did."

"Did this make the naughty prince behave himself?" asked Michael.

"If Mom or Dad spanked Melissa for your mistakes, would it make you behave any better?"

"Well," Michael hesitated. "Melissa is my sister. I think I'd want to behave, knowing she would receive the punishment I deserved."

Jason nodded in agreement. "I feel the same way, but in this story the prince seems to be happiest when his whipping boy is being punished."

"He must have been very cold and cruel," Michael

answered. "If he'd feel the whip himself, I think he'd have a change of heart."

"Have you read this story?" Jason asked in surprise, "because that is exactly what happens to this proud prince. He is mistaken for his own whipping boy and receives the punishment he'd deserved for so long."

Whether the whipping boy idea worked or not, I think we'd all agree it was a very unfair practice. A person should be punished for his or her own mistakes. You might be very surprised to hear, then, that you, too, have your own personal whipping boy. His name is Jesus Christ. Oh, I know we receive punishments from Mom and Dad when we do wrong, but these don't really pay for our sins. The full punishment our sin deserves is eternal death in the fires of hell. Jesus took upon himself this ultimate punishment by becoming a whipping boy for every sinful human being.

Unlike the real whipping boys, who were at times guilty of doing something wrong, Jesus never deserved any punishment. He is holy. He is without sin. He endured the beatings, the thorns, the nails of the cross, and finally his death out of his great love for us. He didn't want us to suffer the pains we really deserved.

Does your heart melt when you hear how Jesus suffered the actual punishment of hell for you? The thought of the cruel pain he endured makes us want to fall down on our knees and thank him for loving us so. Never do we want to be like the proud prince in the story of *The Whipping Boy*, happy and content in our own naughtiness. Who of us could bear God's full anger, if he would make us the whipping boys and girls we deserve to be?

Let us ask God to turn our cold hearts into believing, feeling hearts, praising God for making his own Son Jesus a whipping boy for us!

Prayer: Dear Jesus, thank you for being my whipping boy and taking the punishment I deserve. Let me never despise your death on the cross by making light of my sin. Amen.

Jesus Christ Died For All

Do not gloat when your enemy falls; when he stumbles, do not let your heart rejoice. (Proverbs 24:17)

The rain was only sprinkling when Michael Anderson hurried in from delivering his papers. "What is so funny?" Lindsay asked, when Michael sat down to the breakfast table. "Do you enjoy delivering papers in the rain?"

"I'd enjoy anything today," Michael grinned. "It was a classic morning. I had the pleasure of witnessing Sam Plath cry."

"Are you talking about the boy who is always so mean to you?" Melissa asked, "the boy who collected from your customers and then kept the money?"

Michael nodded. "Today he was blubbering like a baby," he grinned.

"Is Sam the same boy who swiped your papers after you stuffed all the inserts into them?" Lindsay asked.

"He's the one," Michael answered. "And today he certainly got what he deserved for all the grief he's caused me!"

"What happened?" asked Dad.

"We had special inserts again today. Just as he picked up his bundle, they all came untied. The wind caught the sheets and the rain poured on the rest. He's probably still stuffing soggy inserts into his papers, and Mr. Brim is probably still yelling at him. I can't wait to see his face when we get to school."

"Michael," Mrs. Anderson began, "we should never be happy about another person's troubles."

"Well, Sam Plath certainly doesn't care about *my* feelings. He's always making fun of me. Besides, I didn't make his papers fly away and get wet."

"Did you help pick them up?"

"Well, no," Michael frowned, "but he's never lifted a finger to help me either!"

"Still, God wants us to be kind, even to our enemies," Dad reminded him. "Even though we often act like God's enemies by sinning every day, he never stops loving and forgiving us.

64

Through Jesus, he always calls us his friends."

"Instead of laughing at Sam when he is down, why not try to be his friend? A friendship is never made by getting even."

As Michael got ready for school, he thought about how impossible a friendship with Sam would be. How good it felt finally to get revenge on his long-time enemy! As Michael grabbed his school books, he passed the Lenten poster he had made in Sunday School. At the bottom were printed the words: "Jesus Christ died for Michael."

Michael's shoes seemed to be glued to the floor. Why had Jesus died for him? He blushed to think of the time he'd stolen a candy bar from Ruthie's corner grocery store. Ruthie had accepted his apology and hadn't told his dad. Then there was the time he accidentally shoved Jenna Roberts into the drinking fountain and chipped her tooth. And how could he forget the long afternoon in the principal's office, after drawing a funny cartoon of his teacher?

From using curse words he had learned on the bus, to lying, stealing, and cheating, he had done it all! Suddenly Michael's record didn't look any better than Sam's. Yet, he'd been forgiven by those around him, and, more importantly, Jesus had forgiven him, too.

Michael stood before his poster in silence. Miss Grant had told his class to take Jesus' death *personally*. Well, if Jesus died for Michael, personally, he had also died for Sam.

When Michael hopped on his bike that morning, he was determined to make it a classic day—but for a different reason. Instead of laughing at Sam when he was down, he'd help him finish his paper route before school. Michael was eager to witness Sam's astonished face when he tried a little friendship on him. After all, if Jesus died for Michael Anderson, he had died for tough-guy, Sam Plath, too!

Prayer: Dear Jesus, you know how difficult it is for me to love my enemies. Please remind me of all the times you have forgiven the wrong I have done, so I will show the same love to my enemies. Amen.

How Much Did You Cost?

For there is one God and one mediator between God and men, the man Christ Jesus, who gave himself as a ransom for all men. (1 Timothy 2:5,6)

Mrs. Anderson and her daughters, Tracy and Melissa, walked slowly between the store counters which were piled high with Easter candy. From jelly beans to marshmallow eggs, Mom carefully checked the prices marked on each bag before dropping one into her cart.

"Four dollars apiece!" Mom cried. She picked up a beautifully wrapped chocolate bunny. "I can hardly believe it. Who'd pay four dollars for this?"

"I would," Melissa admitted. "It's a lot of money, but no price is too high for a chocolate-lover like me!" she grinned.

"And me, too," little Tracy piped in. "I'd save allowance money for a whole month to have that." Her eyes glistened with delight.

Mrs. Anderson liked chocolate, but not as much as her sweet-toothed daughters.

Everything has a price and no price seems too high if you want something badly enough. For instance, parents whose child has been kidnapped would pay almost any price to have their child returned. No ransom would seem too high.

Now, let's pretend for a moment that *you've* been put on display on one of the counters in the store. Suppose God was doing the shopping. What kind of price would he be willing to pay for you?

Before God's all-seeing eyes it is impossible to hide our faults behind beautiful clothing, clean hair, and a bright smile. God sees everything. He sees how we disobey our parents; he sees how we quarrel with our brothers and sisters; he hears our complaints about homework and household chores. He sees how we cheat on tests, steal, lie, and gossip. God sees right through us like an X-ray camera. Our sin dis-

gusts and saddens him. It makes us enemies of our holy and just God.

Still, God wanted to buy us! And we didn't come cheap. The price on our heads was so high because we owed payment in hell for millions and millions of sins. No amount of money could have bought us back from the power of the devil.

God knew the blood of his holy Son, Jesus, had to be spilled in order to pay for us. It was the highest ransom ever demanded of any father. But our heavenly Father wanted and loved us so much that he was willing to pay the price and give up his own dear Son.

May our hearts be filled with true thanksgiving to our God this Easter. Jesus gave up his own life for ours, even when we weren't worth a dime!

Prayer: Dear Jesus, I'm sorry for all of my sins. Thank you for being the ransom which bought me back from the devil. I will praise and bless your holy name forever. Amen.

Particular

"Martha, Martha," the Lord answered, "you are worried and upset about many things, but only one thing is needed. Mary has chosen what is better, and it will not be taken away from her." (Luke 10:41,42)

Tracy bent carefully over her coloring book. Not a mark slipped over the lines as she let her crayon slide slowly over the picture. She looked up from her page every now and then, keeping an eye on Aunt Catherine's movements.

She smiled to herself, so happy that Mom had let her spend the day with her favorite aunt. She and Tracy were so much alike. "Particular!" Mom said.

"Picky!" Michael said.

Tracy watched as Aunt Catherine straightened each picture and carefully placed the magazines on the coffee table. Aunt Catherine's house was in perfect order. Tracy's room at home was the same way.

"You don't have to stack the pillow cases according to color!" Melissa would scold her. "Who cares if the skates are lined up according to sizes?" Lindsay would ask.

"Are we particular?" Tracy asked Aunt Catherine. "Or are we just picky as Michael always says?"

"Opinions would differ on that point," Aunt Catherine answered with a smile. "An orderly house makes me feel more comfortable. But whether a house is messy or neat, the important thing is to be particular about what really matters."

Tracy thought for a moment. "If I don't want to get a cavity, I should be particular about brushing my teeth. If I don't want to get sick, I should be particular about washing my hands."

Aunt Catherine nodded. "We should be particular about taking care of our bodies. Sad to say, however, many folks are only particular about *this* life. Their life after death doesn't seem to concern them."

"Why aren't people particular about the really important things?" asked Tracy.

"A person can get so wrapped up in his earthy life, living for this moment. Satan tries to rock us to sleep by using all the "particulars" of this life, hoping we'll forget about how much we need Jesus. But Jesus wants us to take time each day to think about the wrong we've done. He wants us to feel truly sorry for all the times we've broken his commandments. He wants us to come often to him in prayer, asking forgiveness for our sins."

"A messy house wouldn't destroy us," Tracy concluded, "but a heart all messy with sin will put us in hell forever."

"Anyone can be particular," Aunt Catherine repeated, "but what is most important is to be particular about one's soul. If a person is smart, he will be as particular about reading family devotions as he is about watching the nightly news. A person wouldn't think of skipping a day of work or school. Well, God wants us to be even more careful about going to church and hearing his word."

"Picky or particular," Tracy confessed, "if it has to do with Jesus, I don't mind being called by either name."

Prayer: Dear Jesus, forgive me for being concerned and careful only about this life. Help me to live each day as if it were my last, asking forgiveness for my sins. Help me to live according to your will. Take me to heaven, not on account of what I've done, but on account of what you've done for me. Amen.

He's My Brother

Therefore, as we have opportunity, let us do good to all people, especially to those who belong to the family of believers. (Galatians 6:10)

"Melissa? What's wrong?" asked Lindsay, as she squeezed past a crowd of people standing on the busy street corner.

"It's Michael. He started home from school before me. As I was heading home, I heard tires screech." Tears rolled down her cheeks. "I just know it's Michael they put into that ambulance."

Lindsay brushed past the rest of the spectators and peered into the paramedic's van. "Michael?" she screamed.

"No, no, Miss. This little fellow's name is Matthew. If you'll step aside, we'll rush him to the hospital." He made some marks on his clipboard. "Possible fractured skull, broken ribs, leg, and arm. Let's go, boys!" the paramedic shouted.

A wave of relief flowed through Lindsay's body. It wasn't Michael at all—just another boy his age with the same build. As the ambulance pulled away from the curb, she swallowed uneasily. What was she thinking? The blaring siren wasn't a victory call declaring that her own brother was safe. It was still an alarm, signaling that a tragedy had taken place. Another boy had been badly injured.

"Thank God, it's not Michael," Lindsay told Melissa when she stepped back onto the sidewalk. "His name is Matthew. But you know—somewhere, someplace, there is another family, feeling the pain we would have felt if it were our brother Michael."

Unfeeling. Cold. Uncaring. Those words describe every one of us. When tragedy strikes, we often sigh with relief, "At least it didn't happen to my family."

Remember, God our heavenly Father cares deeply for all of us. There is no orphan, no stranger, no dark skin, no light skin, no girl, no boy, not worth his time and energy. With him we are all family. He cares deeply for each of us.

This special kind of love is what prompted God to save us. He rescued us from eternal death through his son Jesus, who died on the cross to pay for our sins. This is how much he loves all of us. We are like family to him.

Are you able to love in this special way? Are kids you know too poor, too ugly, too weird, or just too dumb for you to bother with? God's love teaches us to care for each other. Whatever differences there are shouldn't matter. He makes us realize that if it weren't for him, we'd all be lost forever and forced to face punishment in hell when we die.

That night Lindsay and Melissa included a special prayer for little Matthew. He wasn't Michael, but, as a child who trusted in Jesus, he was their brother, and God was his Father, too.

Prayer: Dear Jesus, forgive me for thinking one skin color is better than another. Forgive me for thinking smart people are best. Show me how special all of us are to you. Help me to spread the good news about you, Jesus, my Savior, to all of them! Amen.

Sloppy Work!

Slaves, obey your earthly masters in everything; and do it, not only when their eye is on you and to win their favor, but with sincerity of heart and reverence for the Lord. Whatever you do, work at it with all your heart, as working for the Lord, not for men. (Colossians 3:22,23)

"Finished already?" Mom asked Melissa, as she slipped off the piano bench.

Melissa nodded cautiously. "May I walk over to Carol's? I set the table and finished my homework, too!"

"I wouldn't let her go," a voice announced from across the living room. "She nearly assaulted me with the silverware as she threw it on the table," Melissa's twin brother chuckled.

Melissa glared at Michael. "I didn't throw it on!"

"Then it must have taken a very powerful wind to get the table to look so messy!"

"Mom!" complained Melissa. "Tell Michael to stop teasing me. I set the table, did my homework, and practiced piano. Three jobs finished. Doesn't that count for anything?"

"Sometimes, Melissa, the *way* you complete a task is just as important as getting the job done! Have you forgotten who it is you are working for?" Mom asked.

"Well, Mom, *you* told me to do all those jobs."

"It was for me, in part, but I was thinking of someone else."

"For myself?" asked Melissa.

"In part," Mom replied.

Melissa smiled. "For Jesus?" she asked.

Mom nodded. "Every time you do a task, you should ask yourself what Jesus would think of it."

"Sometimes I wouldn't want him to see any of the work I've done!"

"I suppose it's because we know we can't fool him."

Melissa laughed. "I can't even fool Michael."

Mom smiled. "Even if we *were* able to fool our parents and family, Jesus knows whether or not we are using the talents he has given us to the best of our ability."

"I don't want to waste my talents, but sometimes I don't feel like doing a job carefully. I just want to get it finished."

"Everyone feels that way sometimes. That is when we should use Jesus as our perfect example. We should remember it wasn't only Jesus' death on the cross that saved us, but the perfect life he led, too."

"Just think of it!" Michael exclaimed. "Everything Jesus started and finished was the best it could be."

"But we could never hope to match Jesus' goodness," answered Melissa. "Even my best will never be as good as his."

"True," Mom answered. "This is why we are so thankful it isn't our best which makes heaven ours, but it is Jesus' best. Jesus is our only ticket into heaven. By trying to do our best, we simply show just how much we appreciate all he has done for us."

"Is it possible to thank Jesus even in *little* things, like setting the table?" asked Melissa. "And playing the piano?"

Mom nodded and smiled, "In the little things, in the big things, in all things, we show Jesus just how much we love him."

Prayer: Dear Jesus, I am sorry I often do a job sloppily and halfheartedly. Thank you for doing every job you were given, perfectly. Give me a stronger faith to show I love you, in all things. Amen.

He's So Bad

Everyone who sins breaks the law; in fact, sin is law-lessness. **(1 John 3:4)**

Mrs. Anderson carefully drove her car down the street toward the grocery store. "Look at all the pickets," Michael called from the back seat. "What do you suppose they are protesting?"

"My friend Marie lives on this street. She told me the vacant house on the corner is being renovated. They want to use it as a half-way house."

"What is a half-way house?" asked Michael.

"It is a place where prisoners can go to live when they have just been released from the penitentiary," Lindsay explained. "They live there for a while before they are allowed to go back to their own homes."

"Do you mean prisoners who have killed people?" gasped Melissa.

"And robbed people?" asked Tracy.

"Even drug dealers?" asked Michael. "No wonder those people are picketing. Who wants such bad people living in their neighborhood?"

"Many of these pickets don't want their own children being influenced by these ex-cons," Mom answered.

"I think Marie's parents are the only ones not protesting the half-way house," Lindsay explained. "Marie said it was a hard decision for her parents to make, but they felt that they wanted to give these convicts a second chance. Marie's parents think their neighbors have forgotten the many times when they've also broken the law by driving drunk, smoking pot, shoplifting, or cheating on taxes.

"It certainly takes courage and honesty to admit we are no better than the people who have been caught breaking the law," Mom agreed.

"I still think living next door to a murderer would make my skin crawl!" Melissa gasped.

"What about sleeping in the same room with a sister who hates her classmate?" asked Lindsay.

Melissa frowned. "If you are talking about Laurie Willis, I really don't *hate* her. We're just not speaking. She put a dead toad in my gym shoes, you know."

"Even so, I doubt if you've really forgiven her if you refuse to talk to her. And if we hate another person, it's the same as murder in God's eyes," Lindsay reminded her sister.

"Mom?" asked Melissa. "Is Lindsay hinting I deserve to go to prison because I'm still angry with Laurie?"

"I think Lindsay is trying to make us all realize how any sin breaks God's holy law. In that sense, it puts us in the same category with murderers, thieves, and coveters. Now our government, of course, doesn't put little girls into prison for just hating another person. Yet, the sin of hate would condemn a person to hell in the same way a murderer is condemned to death or given a life term in prison. You see, the punishment in *this* life is just different," Mom explained.

"Instead of always pointing our fingers at ex-cons, we should remember they too can be forgiven. We should take a look at our own sins and ask God's forgiveness for them," Lindsay added.

The same gospel which has changed your heart to trust in Jesus' forgiveness can also change the heart of a convict or ex-convict. Jesus' blood was spilled once for all when he died on the cross. May God, in Christ, wipe away our fears of bringing this message of the cross to those in prison, or to those who have just been released.

Prayer: Dear Jesus, forgive me when I am tempted to think I am so much better than a convict. Help me to bring your word to them as it was bought to me. I know you have the power to change the heart of a hardened criminal even as you have changed mine. Amen.

Just Because He Loves Me

Endure hardship as discipline; God is treating you as sons. For what son is not disciplined by his father? (Hebrews 12:7)

"Do you feel a little better?" Mom asked Melissa as she removed the cool cloth from her daughter's fiery head. Melissa tried to smile as she nodded her pounding head. "You sure are a good little patient, Melissa. I haven't heard a moan or a groan out of you all morning."

Melissa nodded weakly. "I really have no right to complain when I deserve to be sick."

"How do you mean?" asked Mom.

Melissa took a deep breath. "Last Saturday when Shannon Cass got the flu, I laughed about it."

Mom frowned. "Why would you be so uncaring?"

"Shannon invited our whole class except me to her birthday party. Then she had to cancel her party when she got sick."

Mom nodded knowingly. "You were angry because Shannon hadn't invited you, weren't you?"

"But it wasn't right to laugh," Melissa admitted. "I feel sorry I did it. Now I know exactly how Shannon felt, because I had to miss our field trip today. How hard it must have been for Shannon to miss her whole birthday. I do wish God would have been a little easier on me, though. Our class went to the circus, you know."

Mom nodded. "God's way of discipline is sometimes hard to bear. It reminds me of the tough-love many people are talking about these days. God has to be tough and hard on us sometimes to remind us to feel sorry for our sins."

"I wonder what life would be like without these little reminders," Melissa sighed, rubbing her tired eyes.

"Oh, I think it would be very easy to be careless about the bad things we do. If we never had any pain or troubles, we might forget just how much we need a Savior. What do you think would happen to you if Dad and I would never punish you when you did something wrong?"

"I might begin to feel that it doesn't matter how I act," Melissa reasoned. "But you love me, and you want me to learn to keep the rules at home. That way, later on, when I get out on my own, I will also learn to keep the laws of our country. You don't want me to wind up in jail some day."

"It is the same way with God. He doesn't want us to wind up in hell some day. With every trouble or pain or trial, he is reminding us to cling to him. He doesn't want us to live only for this life, but for the life that is to come as well."

Melissa smiled. "Then when trouble comes to us, we really shouldn't worry. We know Jesus truly cares about us."

Mom smiled and pulled a small envelope from her apron pocket. "This is for you, Melissa. It came in this morning's mail."

Melissa carefully opened the tiny envelope. "It's an invitation to Shannon's birthday party," she announced in a bewildered voice. Melissa read the note aloud:

"Dear Melissa,
   I know you've been out of school for two days now, but I do hope you will be better by Saturday for my party. When Tanya told me I'd forgotten to invite you the first time, I felt really rotten. Please get well, Melissa, so you can come.

Your friend,
Shannon Cass"

"I had no right at all to feel badly toward Shannon," Melissa confessed. "I really don't deserve this invitation. Why is God so good to me, when I've been so unfeeling toward Shannon?"

Mom rose and patted Melissa's arm. "It is the same question that has puzzled sinful human beings ever since Adam and Eve fell into sin. God is love, Melissa. I guess that explains it all!"

Prayer: Dear Jesus, thank you for showing your great love for me by disciplining me when I need it. Let my troubles bring me that much closer to you. Amen.

Practice Makes Perfect

If you hold to my teaching, you are really my disciples. Then you will know the truth, and the truth will set you free. (John 8:31,32)

Jason laid his Confirmation workbook in his lap and yawned. "I will be so relieved when I am able to put all this Catechism studying behind me!"

Lindsay looked up from her book and smiled. "Just wait until you hear Pastor Miles' pre-confirmation 'sermon.' With every class he stresses how our instruction has only just begun!"

"Not for me!" Jason answered. "Once I close my Catechism, it's closed for good!"

"Hey, Jason!" Michael called from the dining room. "How about warming up for your baseball game with a little game of catch?"

"Sure," Jason responded eagerly. He jumped out of his chair, laid his Catechism aside, and hurried through the dining room. He stopped short. Dad sat at the table paying the monthly bills. Jason wondered if he had heard his comments.

"I don't think you need to practice for today's game," Dad began nonchalantly. "You guys did so well a week ago."

Jason frowned. "Dad, I could lose my accuracy in less than a week if I stop practicing my pitching. Coach says winning depends on how well you get ready for the game."

"Hmmm," Dad murmured, "if that is true about baseball, I wonder if it is also true about God's word. I wonder what would happen to a person's faith if after Confirmation he never opened a Catechism or Bible again."

Jason's mouth was dry. His dad *had* heard his foolish comments! "I suppose a guy would forget most of what he had learned." Jason paused. "I didn't mean to say I don't like Catechism classes. I do like reading the Bible, but the memorization and worksheets are just so much work!"

Dad nodded. "If you want what you've learned to make a difference in your life, the Bible and Catechism must stay open throughout your life." Your study should never stop. This is true about school or any business. Take Mom, for instance. If she wants to keep her nursing license, she must keep studying and taking tests. There is no time when she can just close the book and stop learning. She wants to be prepared to face every new problem on the job."

"But, Dad, I'll always believe Jesus is my Savior. Nothing could make me doubt that."

"Those were your Uncle Jeff's exact words to Grandma before he went off to a state college. There he met a teacher who didn't believe God even existed."

"Now Uncle Jeff doesn't believe much of anything either," Jason admitted.

"Going to a public college has its built-in dangers, because students aren't surrounded by Christians all the time. But perhaps Uncle Jeff wouldn't have been led astray by unchristian teachers if he'd have kept his Bible open more often."

Jason looked at the floor. "I think I've been taking my Catechism classes for granted."

"Neglecting God's word is the most dangerous way to live, Jason. You know baseball takes practice. It is no different with God's word. If you want to be a good pitcher, you must work on your pitch; if you want your faith to remain strong . . ."

"You must keep your Bible open," Jason finished, "even after you have been confirmed!" he grinned sheepishly.

Prayer: Dear Jesus, forgive me for getting tired of studying your word. Help me fight the devil who wants to pull me away from you. Give me a strong desire to study your word at all times. Amen.

God's Recipes

Christ is the end of the law so that there may be righteousness for everyone who believes. **(Romans 10:4)**

Jason, Michael, and Tracy tumbled excitedly into the kitchen. "Are your cookies ready yet?" Jason called. "We're starved!"

Proudly Melissa pushed the dish of golden brown cookies toward her brothers and sister. Eagerly they helped themselves. After one bite, however, their smiles vanished, and their squeals turned into groans and complaints.

"How did your cookies turn out?" asked Mom, who appeared just then at the kitchen door.

"They don't like them!" Melissa wailed in disappointment.

Mom frowned. "Why not? They look lovely to me." Mrs. Anderson bit into a cookie and rolled the morsel around in her mouth. She coughed. "Are you *sure* these are ginger cookies?"

Melissa nodded. "I followed the recipe exactly." She paused. "Except we were out of cinnamon, so I substituted something called paprika for it."

"Paprika?" echoed Mom, "in ginger cookies? I usually add paprika to soup and egg dishes." Mom took another tiny bite. "Ginger cookies are usually so sweet, but these . . ."

"Well," Melissa hesitated, "we were out of molasses and I could find only one-half cup of sugar."

"What did you substitute for the molasses and sugar?"

"Nothing. I left out the rest of the sweetener. I didn't think anyone would notice."

"We noticed! We noticed!" came a flurry of voices.

Have you ever tried to bake something? The first rule every good cook learns is to follow a recipe exactly as it is written. Melissa's cookies were spoiled because she forgot this important rule.

You could say the Bible is like a recipe book. It is filled with the ingredients of God's recipe for heaven. The first ingredient is called the law. Law passages in the Bible show us our sin. The other ingredient in God's recipe for heaven is called the gospel. These gospel passages tell us that Jesus came into the world to keep the law for us. He also died on the cross to pay for the sins we have committed.

These are very simple ingredients; yet sinful human beings think they know better than God about the recipe for heaven. For instance, God says that sin is bad. It condemns us to hell. But some people argue, "Since God is love, he would never punish anyone in hell!" Others don't want to follow the part of God's recipe which says that only through his Son Jesus will anyone be saved. They disagree and say, "Oh, but look at my life! I'm not so bad. Some of the good things I've done will help me get into heaven!"

These ideas make good *human sense*, but not good *God sense*. What God says, he means. He doesn't want his recipe changed. We can't get to heaven by using just the one ingredient called the law. Trying to keep the law—the good we do—isn't good enough. It can't make up for the bad things we've done, and it won't open the doors of heaven for us.

If you want ginger cookies, you have to use ginger, cinnamon, and all the ingredients the recipe calls for. If you want to get into heaven, you must admit you aren't good enough to make it there on your own. You must include the gospel ingredient which lovingly declares your sins forgiven through Jesus Christ.

The Bible tells us, "Believe on the Lord Jesus, and you will be saved" (Acts 16:31). When you believe, you are following God's recipe exactly!

Prayer: Dear Jesus, please forgive me when I am tempted to think I can somehow make up for my own sins. Help me to realize that heaven can be mine only when I trust in you as my only Savior. Help me never to change your word. Amen.

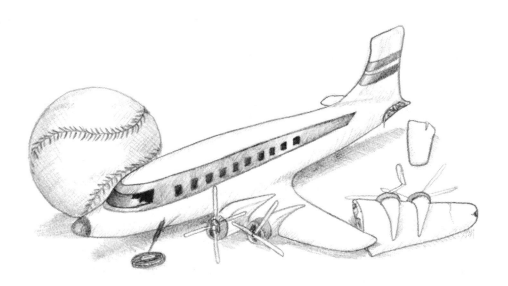

Not By Ourselves

But the fruit of the Spirit is love, joy, peace, patience, kindness, goodness, faithfulness, gentleness, and self-control. Against such things there is no law. (Galatians 5:22,23)

Jason was seated at the card table in the garage busily gluing together a model airplane. He had the wings in place and was ready to put the windows in. But the small plastic pieces kept falling into the cockpit instead of sticking tightly to the window frames.

"I give up," he shouted in frustration. "I'll never get these on!"

With blinding fury, Jason threw the whole airplane to the side of the garage. Seeing the broken plane smashed on the cement hadn't cooled his anger in the least. His dad had been reminding him to watch his temper. But when he failed at something, his temper burned like a fire inside of him.

Through the open garage door Mr. Anderson saw the entire scene. He walked into the garage and picked up the broken airplane. He pulled up a chair beside his son and reached for the tube of airplane glue.

Before long, Dad had repaired the damages. The broken wing was once again glued into place, and the wing's propellers were spinning smoothly. Finally, Dad began to tackle the small windows. As he waited for them to dry, he looked into his son's bewildered face.

"It looks like this airplane's life was almost cut short," Dad finally spoke.

"I'm sorry I blew up again, Dad," Jason confessed. "The more I try to control my temper, the more it controls me."

"Maybe that's because you're trying to control it all by yourself. God tells us that the fruit of the Spirit is self-control. Trying to control our anger without the Holy Spirit's help doesn't work, even though we may pretend that everything is under control."

"I guess that's what I've been doing," Jason answered. "Yesterday I tried really hard to watch my temper. When Tracy tied my shoelaces into knots, I calmly untied them. When some of my friends at school stuffed spitballs into the keyhole of my locker, I picked every last one of them out without raising my voice. Even this morning when Michael used the last of the hot water for one of his marathon showers, I kept quiet and took a cold one. Through it all I was steaming mad, but I just didn't show it. Gluing the airplane's small windows in place was more than I could handle alone."

"That is exactly the point, Jason," Mr. Anderson answered. "God doesn't want you to handle your problems alone. You kept your temper inside, and it naturally had to explode. God is the one who gives us self-control by taking our anger away."

"Do you mean I can be patient on the inside as well as the outside?"

Mr. Anderson nodded. "Patience doesn't come by accident. God's Spirit has all the power to push your anger out of you and give you patience, but your faith which trusts in Jesus as your Savior needs to be refueled, to be strengthened every day with the word of God."

Jason nodded and smiled. "With God's help, I'll then be able to throw my anger, instead of model airplanes, out the window."

Jason couldn't finish the airplane without his father's help. Now he realized he couldn't control his anger without his heavenly Father's help either. When we forget to study God's word, our faith becomes weak, and we find ourselves without the weapons to fight our anger. The fruits of the Spirit can be ours if we stay close to God's word through family devotions and Bible reading. Through them all the fruits of the Spirit can belong to us.

Prayer: Dear Jesus, please forgive me when anger flares up inside me. Give me self-control so that I may be patient with those around me. Amen.

Zap It, Lord

We always thank God for all of you, mentioning you in our prayers. We continually remember before our God and Father your work produced by faith, your labor prompted by love, and your endurance inspired by hope in our Lord Jesus Christ. (1 Thessalonians 1:2)

Two fat tears slowly trickled down to Tracy's lip, trembled there a moment, and fell, plop, on the floor of the front porch. "Will God make Mrs. Ritmore well?" she asked her mother, as they watched the paramedics carry their neighbor out on a stretcher and carefully set her into the ambulance. Tracy remembered how every afternoon, sunshiny or cloudy, the elderly lady had invited her in for a snack after kindergarten was over. How she missed Mrs. Ritmore's loving attention already!

Mom knelt beside her youngest daughter. "This is the second time Mrs. Ritmore has fallen on her hip. It may take quite some time for the bone to heal. We must pray that God will let it heal properly."

"But why does it have to take so long?" asked Tracy. "Why doesn't God just zap that bone together like he did in some of his miracles?"

"When he lived on earth, Jesus performed most of his miracles to prove he was God's Son and our Savior. These days God often uses quiet miracles instead of a quick zap."

"But why?" persisted Tracy. "Mrs. Ritmore will have to stay in the hospital for weeks and weeks. She'll have to go through so much pain while the bone heals. Wouldn't it be more loving of God to heal her right now?"

"We have to trust God to know what is best for Mrs. Ritmore's soul. He doesn't enjoy seeing any of us suffer, but very often when we are faced with much pain, it makes us trust Jesus and his power of forgiveness and healing all the more."

"So while her body is getting stronger, her faith will too," Tracy answered. "But, how is it better for *me* to have to wait so long for Mrs. Ritmore to come home? Doesn't God understand how much I'll miss her?"

"Oh, God understands more than you realize. When someone's sick or in pain, it gives you a chance to show just how much you do love and appreciate that person. You see, if God would always zap away our problems, it wouldn't give the doctors, nurses, friends, and neighbors a chance to show their faith in Jesus by the way they help."

Tracy's eyes brightened with understanding. "Up to now, Mrs. Ritmore has always been doing something for me. Finally, I have a chance to do something for her."

Zap! Zap! Zap! How many of us haven't thought exactly as little Tracy? If only God would zap away all sickness and troubles, we would live in a perfect world, not bothered by so much sadness. If zapping our problems away would be the best for all of us, God would do it, but he knows that what seems the easiest way isn't always the best way for us.

By giving us a chance to serve each other in our troubles, sickness, and disappointments, he gives us an opportunity to show our thankfulness to him for his suffering and death on the cross. By giving us a chance to get closer to people's needs, he also gives us an opportunity to tell them Jesus died for their sins, too. Instead of God doing all the zapping to fill people's needs, he graciously allows us to be his faithful "miracle workers."

Prayer: Dear Jesus, when those I love are in pain, I feel so sad. Please make their pain turn out for good. Increase my faith as well as the faith of the one who is sick. Help me to use my love for you to serve those in pain and in trouble. Amen.

I Had This Dream

The secret things belong to the LORD our God, but the things revealed belong to us and to our children forever, that we may follow all the words of this law. (Deuteronomy 29:29)

"Melissa won't get up, Mom," Lindsay complained. "She says she's too sick to go to school." Lindsay cupped a hand over her lips to hide her smile. "She's convinced she's dying of cancer."

"I wouldn't laugh at you if you were dying," came the hurt reply from beneath the covers. "Cancer is nothing to giggle about."

"Cancer is a serious disease," Mom agreed, brushing her hand across Melissa's forehead. "But why do you think you have it?"

Without a word, Melissa drew out a very worn paperback from under her pillow. "Carol gave me this yesterday. It's a book about dreams."

"Melissa has had the same dream for the past two weeks," Lindsay explained. "In each dream she gets cancer and dies."

"The book says dreams which return night after night often come true," Melissa explained. "The writer is a psychologist, Mom. He understands the human mind."

"I know an even more reliable author. He understands the mind better than any psychologist," Mom answered.

"Who is it?" asked Melissa.

"Silly, Mom is talking about the one who *made* our minds," Lindsay told her sister. She handed her mother the small Bible setting on the desk.

"God tells us in Deuteronomy 29:29 that the secret things belong to him. It is impossible to know if a dream is truly from God or the devil or our own sinful minds," Mom explained. "Most dreams come from our daily thoughts, Melissa. If something made a terrific impression on you during the day, you usually dream about it at night."

Lindsay's eyes opened wide. "What about Karen Wilke? Isn't she the one in your class who has cancer?"

Melissa nodded. "Last week she did a report on her cancer in front of the class. I just know I have cancer like Karen," Melissa sobbed.

"Don't you see?" asked Mom. "It is very possible you have been dreaming about Karen's cancer, not your own!"

The flow of tears stopped suddenly. "Do you really think so? Are you saying I may not be dying after all?"

"Not at the moment," Mom grinned, "but we all must face our death some day. Looking into a dream book isn't the way to handle our worries."

"Using a dream book is really like reading your horoscope to find out the future, isn't it?" said Lindsay.

Mom nodded. "The devil uses these nightmares to make us doubt God's promises to watch over us."

"Why hasn't the devil been able to make Karen upset, even though she knows she truly has cancer?"

"Karen's a believer, Melissa. She trusts that God will be with her through any kind of sickness. Even if she does die, she is confident she will be with Jesus in heaven. She trusts that he has paid for her sins on the cross. *Death* can't even make her afraid."

"And if I should get sick and die, I will be safe in Jesus' arms, too," Melissa smiled. "I wonder why I was so afraid."

"Because you've been reading the wrong kind of books," Lindsay answered, tossing the offending paperback into the wastebasket.

Melissa grinned and threw back the quilt. "Somehow I don't think I'll be bothered with the same dream tonight!"

Mom handed her daughter the tiny Bible. "Filling your mind with God's promises is the best way to put all nightmares to sleep!"

Prayer: Dear Jesus, sometimes my bad dreams frighten me. Remind me I have nothing to fear because you took away all my sins on the cross. Amen.

Vacation From God's Word?

Your promises have been thoroughly tested, and your servant loves them. (Psalm 119:140)

Michael Anderson snuggled down deep into the covers. He relaxed his toes against the coolness of the sheets. Giving his pillow a satisfying punch, he nestled his head deeply into the feathery down.

"Ah!" he thought, "nothing in the world is better than summer vacation."

Just as Michael had drifted from consciousness, he slipped back into reality. Mom hurried into the room, flipped the shades up, brushed his forehead with a kiss and laid his freshly-pressed suit at the bottom of the bed.

"Hurry, Michael," she coaxed, "get washed and dressed or we'll be late for church."

Michael blinked his eyes in wonderment. "But, Mom, it's summer vacation."

Mrs. Anderson sat down beside her son and smiled. "That's vacation from school, not church," she laughed.

Melissa appeared in the doorway and piped in, "Lots of people do take a vacation from church during the summer months. It's a good thing God doesn't take a vacation from us!"

Mom nodded. "He still sends rain and sunshine and supplies us with food and clothing. If he'd take a vacation from us for even a few minutes, we would die."

Michael nodded. "We couldn't even breathe without him. Pastor told us he holds our whole universe together. We'd go flying out into space if God didn't use his power to hold us down!" Michael giggled.

"Sometimes, going to church seems like a drudgery because we are sinful human beings," Mom continued. "When we feel this way, it shows just how much we need to be reminded of what sinners we are and how much we need Jesus' forgiveness."

"Billy McGiver's dad likes to go fishing on Sundays in the summer. He says that's when the fish are biting the best. Is he sinning?"

"God hasn't commanded us to worship on any certain day the way he did with the children of Israel. Their holy day was the Sabbath, or Saturday. We worship on Sundays, because that is the day Jesus rose from the dead," Mom explained.

"Then any day we choose to worship would make God happy," Lindsay answered, poking her head into the room.

Mom nodded. "Now, I don't know whether or not the fish bite better on Sundays, but I do know God doesn't want us to despise his word. He also wants us to worship with other Christians if we possibly can."

"Some churches have services on Wednesday or another night during the week," Michael announced.

"Well, what about when we go camping?" Melissa asked. "Are we despising God's word when we miss church?"

"But we can't go," Michael complained. "There are no churches for miles around. Dad said so."

Mom smiled. "We can't go to church then, and that's why we have our own church at the campsite."

Melissa's eyes sparkled. "Outdoor church is fun!"

"Dad likes it, too," Lindsay nodded. "He says it's the only time he gets to preach the sermon!"

This summer when we rest our bodies and minds from the usual hectic pace of school and work, let us all find true rest in the pages of God's Word. Whether we're at a campsite or at a cabin by the lake or on the road, let us make sure our Savior is along. We need his saving grace just as much in the summer as at any other time of the year!

Prayer: Dear Jesus, help me to be like your disciples long ago who rejoiced to worship you in your house. Forgive me when I think I need a rest from your word. Amen.

I'm Sorry, I Believe

If we confess our sins, he is faithful and just and will forgive us our sins and purify us from all unrighteousness. (1 John 1:9)

"Tracy," Mom called from the flower bed, "I told you never to cross the street without asking."

Tracy cautiously walked across the grass toward Mom. "Dolly crossed the street without asking," she excused herself.

"But I told you not to cross our busy street alone."

"But Dolly crossed alone," Tracy insisted.

"But what about you, Tracy?"

"What about Dolly?"

"We aren't talking about Dolly; we are talking about you!"

"But Dolly crossed, too, without asking," Tracy insisted.

"I think you may be on a dead-end, one-way street with this one," Dad told Mom as he stepped off the front porch. He pulled his five-year-old daughter to him. "Tracy, Mom and I want you to stop blaming others for *your* mistakes."

"But if Dolly did wrong, too, I don't want to be the only one in trouble," Tracy answered.

"No one does," agreed Dad. "But when we sin, whether it was our idea or not, we must pay the consequences. Let's take crossing the street, for instance. If you and Dolly crossed the street and a car hit only you, who would be dead?"

"I guess I would, Daddy."

"Would blaming Dolly bring you back to life, even if she *told* you to cross the street?"

"No, if you're dead, you're dead. Nothing can change that!"

"Remember how the devil in the garden of Eden tempted Eve to eat the fruit God commanded Adam and Eve not to eat?"

Tracy nodded. "Eve talked Adam into trying it too."

"Was Adam less guilty than Eve was?"

"No, God punished them both. Adam had to work very hard in the fields, and Eve had much pain when she had a baby because they both sinned."

"So, even though Eve sinned first and tempted Adam to sin, they both were punished."

Tracy nodded. "They both had to die because of their sin."

"Did it do any good for Eve to blame the snake or for Adam to blame Eve?" Dad asked. Tracy shook her head. "Instead of hearing them blaming one another, God wanted to hear from them how sorry they were for disobeying him. And then when God told them he'd send a Savior some day to pay for their sins, God wanted them to believe his promise."

Tracy swallowed uncertainly, noticing how Dad kept looking at her expectantly. "I *am* sorry I crossed the street without asking, Daddy. And, I'm sorry I blamed Dolly for what I did wrong!"

"I'm sorry. I believe." When we sin, this is exactly what God longs to hear from our lips. When we admit our sin, our loving God is immediately available to take our sin away. This is why he sent his Son Jesus into the world. If we push the guilt onto someone else, we act as though we aren't responsible. When we confess our sins, we are ready to have them washed clean through Jesus' blood on the cross. "I'm sorry. I believe." May these be the words God hears when we sin.

Prayer: Dear Jesus, please forgive me for trying to excuse myself when I sin. Instead of blaming others, help me to admit my sin. I believe you paid for all my sins when you died on the cross. Amen.

Losing Sight Of Purpose

"You are a king, then!" said Pilate. Jesus answered, "You are right in saying I am a king. In fact, for this reason I was born, and for this I came into the world, to testify to the truth. Everyone on the side of truth listens to me." (John 18:37)

"What are you doing?" Lindsay asked her younger brother.

"Oh, I'm just recording all the days I'll be mowing lawns this summer," Jason explained.

Lindsay peered over his shoulder and frowned. "But, Jason, you've practically marked the entire calendar full."

"Sure, the word is out about me. I've been hired all over the neighborhood. By the end of the summer, I should be staring at quite a pile of money."

"What do you need with a whole pile of money? I thought you wanted to earn just enough to go on the camping trip."

"I did," Jason agreed.

Another frown appeared on Lindsay's face as she studied the calendar more closely. "Do you realize you've marked the week of the camp-out as well?"

Jason shrugged. "I decided to skip the camp-out this year. If I don't, I'll lose my jobs. Someone else will take my place."

"But the camp-out was the reason you wanted these jobs in the first place," Lindsay persisted.

"I know," Jason admitted, "but the money was too hard to pass up."

Lindsay sighed and rose from her chair. "This discussion is hopeless, Jason. The real trouble here is that you've completely lost sight of your purpose."

Losing sight of one's purpose—that is what Satan tempted Jesus to do. Jesus had come into the world to seek and save those who were lost, to suffer and die on the cross that we might have forgiveness for our sins. That was his purpose. But Satan suggested to him that it was not fitting for the Son of God to suffer and die.

"Take the easy way to achieve your kingdom," he suggested. "Perform a dazzling miracle and the people will become your faithful followers. Or worship me and I'll give you a kingdom of great glory—at no cost to you. Why pay the price of your blood to win it?"

Jesus rejected Satan's suggestions. He chose the way of the cross and he walked that way to the very end, for you and for me and for all. If he'd have lost sight of his purpose for coming into the world, we'd have been lost forever because of our sin.

As Satan constantly tried to tempt Jesus from his purpose and goal in life, he also tries to tempt us away from what really matters in life.

Instead of taking a job simply to provide for our needs, we may get so involved in the urge to earn more money that we become greedy and possibly even forget all about Christ. Instead of buying presents simply to show our love for each other and our Savior at Christmas, we may wind up buying things just to satisfy our own selfish hearts. Instead of bringing Jesus to those who are in need, we may become so busy helping them with food and clothing—good as these things are—that we forget about their greatest need—knowing their Savior.

Thank God that Jesus did not lose sight of his purpose. He went willingly to the cross as our Savior to take away our sins. He obeyed his heavenly Father's will and fulfilled the purpose for which he had come into the world.

Why has God given you your life? Is it to become the richest, the most famous, and the most successful person in the world? All such goals fulfill only our greedy, selfish desire to glorify ourselves.

God's goal and purpose for us is far less flashy. He wants us simply to tell those we meet that Jesus loves them and died for their sins, too. Let nothing distract you from this truly noble and God-pleasing purpose in your life.

Prayer: Dear Jesus, thank you for not losing sight of your purpose in life as I often do. Keep me on the right track so nothing will keep me from trusting in you and bringing your word to others. Amen.

In Peace Or In Punishment?

Therefore, since we have been justified through faith, we have peace with God through our Lord Jesus Christ. (Romans 5:1)

Michael Anderson dangled his legs from the top bunk as he absent-mindedly stared out the upstairs window. The sound of a wailing siren brought him up short. A police car, with its lights flashing, pulled into the driveway of the house next door. A frantic young mother bolted out of the front door, holding her baby in her arms. The baby's face looked almost blue. The policeman grabbed him and began to squeeze his tiny chest. Almost immediately the baby started coughing and wheezing. The mother threw her arms around the policeman, thanking him for saving the life of her son.

What a story Michael had to tell! But just as he jumped from the top bunk, he heard another siren. A second patrol car raced up the street and screeched to a halt in the driveway of the house across the street. Michael heard the sound of breaking glass. A man threw himself out of the side window of the house and the policeman raced to catch him.

Michael gasped. Mrs. Ritmore was on vacation. The suspicious-looking character must have been trying to rob her and tripped the burglar alarm.

In utter amazement, Michael watched this unusual drama unfold. At one house the young mother was thanking the heroic officer with hugs and shouts of delight. Across the street, the policeman wrestled the intruder to the ground, clasped the handcuffs around his wrists, and roughly pulled him into the police car.

Two identical police cars. One woman ran to greet an officer in happiness; one man ran away from an officer in fear and dread. To one, the police car came in love and peace; to the other it came as a threat.

The incident involving the two police cars is very much like the situation we will all witness at the end of the world. To the believers who trust in the Lord Jesus for the forgiveness of sins, Judgment Day will come as a day of rejoicing, a time to rush out and gladly meet the Savior who has promised to take his believers with him to heaven.

To the unbelievers, however, who never thought they needed a Savior, that day will come as a day of fear and distress, for to them Jesus will come as a stern judge who will sentence them forever to the fires of hell.

Just as a policeman *wants* to come only as a helper and protector, so our Savior, Jesus, *wants* to come only in love and forgiveness. To those who repent of their sins and trust in God's gracious forgiveness, there is only one way our Lord Jesus can come, as Savior and friend. May God give us a strong faith so that we always receive him as our Savior! May we always love, honor, and adore him.

Prayer: Dear Jesus, I know I really deserve the punishment you bore on the cross for my sins. I am truly sorry for them all. Come to me only in peace and forgiveness, dear Lord. Amen.

A Happy Ending

Be kind and compassionate to one another, forgiving each other, just as in Christ God forgave you. (Ephesians 4:32)

Lindsay and her cousin Susan sipped the bubbly punch and nibbled at the dainty sweets set before them on the silver tray. From the raised porch they looked across the green lawn at the happy wedding couple.

"I feel like I've been put together with safety pins," Susan whispered.

"Me, too," Lindsay answered. "How could the bridal shop have mixed up our sizes so badly?"

Susan shrugged. "It wouldn't be so bad if this was the only mistake, but it's not. Did you hear? The flower shop delivered the bouquets *five* hours early?"

"I thought they looked pretty droopy," Lindsay replied. "And as though the mistakes about the flowers and the dresses weren't bad enough, did you hear about the wedding cake? Last night half of it landed on the floor because a jiggly table leg collapsed. Aunt Marie was up half the night baking and decorating another cake!"

"What else could possibly go wrong?" said Susan as Lindsay's mother swept into a chair beside them.

Mrs. Anderson didn't speak but continued to dab the bottom of her skirt vigorously. "One of the waiters dropped the punch bowl," she explained finally. "I happened to be in the wrong place at the wrong time!"

Susan looked at Lindsay. Lindsay looked at Susan. "That's what the bride and groom are probably saying to each other right now," Lindsay sighed. "How can they possibly have a happy marriage after such a disastrous wedding?"

Mrs. Anderson smiled. "A disastrous wedding day doesn't mean a disastrous marriage will follow."

"And a perfect wedding doesn't mean it'll be a perfect marriage," Susan reminded her cousin.

"Well, then what really makes a perfect marriage?" asked Lindsay. "Divorces are almost as common as weddings are."

"No marriage is ever perfect," Mom began, "but a strong, loving relationship between husband and wife will certainly help them stand up against the many troubles they'll have to face in their married life."

"Why aren't all marriages strong?" asked Susan. "It seems to me every couple really loves and cares for one another on their wedding day."

"A truly strong marriage depends not only on a couple's love for each other. It also depends on their love for God and whether or not they want him to play an active role in their marriage."

"Some couples think a new house, new furniture, and a fancy car will give them what they need to stay happy," Susan said knowingly.

"They find out soon enough that a lot of money and fancy things won't give them the support they need in times of sickness or trouble, or if one of them loses a job," Lindsay replied.

"Or in the death of a child," Susan added.

"Only God can help them through those kinds of storms," Mrs. Anderson explained. "Only Jesus' self-less suffering and death on the cross can really teach a couple to be forgiving and understanding toward each other. When they know the promise of heaven is theirs in Christ, all their trouble is easier to bear."

"They know, in Christ, there will always be a happy ending," Lindsay added.

Suddenly there was a noisy clatter of breaking glass. The cousins couldn't hide their smiles; each mishap seemed a bit comical after so many others.

"Let's go and greet the bride and groom," Mom suggested suddenly. "I want them to know what a lovely wedding it has been."

"Lovely, Mom? You've got to be kidding!" Lindsay exclaimed.

"Nothing but lovely," Mrs. Anderson said firmly. "A marriage built on Jesus is simply beautiful even after a whole day of disasters!"

Prayer: Dear Lord Jesus, right now, my wedding day seems so very far away. Please guide me in choosing the right marriage partner. Together may we build our marriage around you. Amen.

I Am So Bored

*Because of the L*ORD*'s great love we are not consumed,
for his compassions never fail.* (Lamentations 3:22)

"Am I ever bored!" Melissa groaned, slowly swinging one leg onto the floor.

With a grin, Michael picked up Justin's toy hammer and tapped his twin sister's leg. "Hmmm, maybe we could use you for our new clubhouse."

Melissa swept her leg aside. "I didn't say I was *a* board, as in a stick of wood! I said bored, b-o-r-e-d. Here it's barely the end of July and there's nothing left to do. Oh, I am really bored!" she complained again, dropping her head onto the living room sofa's armrest.

"I believe those were the exact words I spoke more than twenty-five years ago," Mom said, as she rubbed the dust cloth over the coffee table. "It was July then, too. I was tired of my dolls, tired of riding my bike, tired of playing games, tired of everything! And that afternoon was so still: no wind, absolutely nothing was happening on our farm."

"But as quickly as I could snap my fingers, everything changed. The wind picked up. The trees looked as though they were doing deep knee bends. Everything that wasn't nailed down was flying into the air! My dad dashed in from the fields just then. He had spotted a tornado on the horizon. He grabbed us and herded us into the basement."

"Was it a tornado like Dorothy saw in the Wizard of Oz?" gasped Tracy.

"Oh my yes, it was a real honest-to-goodness Kansas tornado, and it was heading straight for our farm."

"It sure put some excitement into a boring summer afternoon!" chuckled Melissa.

Mom's mouth grew sad and solemn. "In seconds we lost both the barn and the house. As we huddled under a heavy table in the basement, the rest of the house above us was just pealed off. With one look we knew we had lost everything. All of our possessions had been demolished. Only our lives had been spared. I knew then I would give anything for just a small piece of boredom once again!"

Melissa shivered. "Do you think God brought that tornado because you had been complaining about how bored you were?"

"We never know exactly why God lets catastrophes happen to us. But we do know that, whatever disasters come, God will turn them into something for our good. I learned that day to count my blessings instead of filling my day with complaints. It was certainly out of his love and mercy that God graciously permitted us to live!"

"So when we are tempted to be bored, one way we can use our free time is to thank God for the mercy he has shown to us." Mom told them.

"We should especially thank him for the love he showed in sending Jesus into the world to die for our sins and for being our Savior," Melissa added.

"Since we all have this boredom problem at one time or another, why don't we make a big collage showing all the blessings God has given to us. Then, when we think we are going to be bored, all we'll have to do is look at the picture we made to remember all God has done for us," Mom said.

Prayer: Dear Jesus, when I am bored, help me to remember all the ways you show your love for me. Help me to remember that "free time" gives me more time to study your word. Amen.

I Don't Have To; I Want To

I rejoiced with those who said to me, "Let us go to the house of the LORD." (Psalm 122:1)

"I'm glad I don't have to get all dressed up on such a hot day and go to church," Bobby Brown jeered from his back porch. "You'd give anything to be free like me, wouldn't you!"

Michael frowned at Bobby's taunts. He dug his toe angrily into the porch. "I am, too, free!" he mumbled, pulling the screen door open and darting inside.

The cool house was filled with the sounds of the Anderson family getting ready for church. Michael followed the sound of Dad's buzzing razor up to the master bathroom. "What'll it be, a shave or just a haircut?" Dad winked down at his son.

"No, Dad," Michael answered, smiling slightly. "What I really need is some information. Am I free? I mean, would you let me decide whether or not I *want to* go to church?"

"Hmmm," Dad murmured. "Has Bobby Brown been giving you a hard time again?" Dad slowly laid his razor into its case.

"Michael, church is not a have-to place. It's a want-to place. No one puts a gun to our backs and forces us to go."

"Then, I could stay home if I wanted to?" asked Michael hopefully.

Dad paused. "Remember the commotion at the supper table last night?"

Michael shrugged. "Sure, little Justin wouldn't eat his carrots. He stuffed them into his bib overalls."

"Did Mom let him get away with it?"

Michael shook his head. "No, she didn't. She mixed a little brown sugar with another helping of carrots and spoon-fed him until they were gone."

"Why doesn't Mom just let Justin decide whether or not he wants to eat carrots? Perhaps by the time he reaches your age he'll acquire a taste for them."

"By my age! What about the time in between? Even I know that his body needs vitamins while he's growing. Justin would be so set in his ways by the time he got as old as I am that he'd probably never touch another vegetable again."

"You see, Michael," Dad smiled, "just as Justin is too young to decide his own dinner menu, you are too young to decide your own spiritual menu. That is one reason God gave you parents—to provide that spiritual menu for you."

What we all have to remember is that *God wants* us to go to church to worship him with our lips and with our lives. And if we just stop a moment to remember what God has done for us, how happy we should be to give him this worship when we know it pleases him."

"In other words," said Michael, "God wants going to church to be an I-want-to instead of I-have-to."

"Exactly Michael," answered Dad.

"Am I still free then, even though I don't decide whether or not I go to church?"

"You are free in an even more important way, Michael. Your sins have been forgiven by Jesus. You are no longer weighed down by them. You no longer are the devil's slave. Sin has no hold on you any more."

Michael looked up at his father thoughtfully. "Dad," he said boldly, "I know I am only ten, but I think I *am* old enough to choose whether or not I want to go to church." Dad raised his eyebrows expectantly. "I am old enough because I pick church, Dad. If God wants me to be in church, that's where I'll be," he grinned.

Prayer: Dear Jesus, sometimes kids make fun of me for going to church. Help me not to be bothered by what they say. I really do like to go. Help me to realize how very important your word is in my life. Amen.

Our Journey Through Life

But you are a chosen people, a royal priesthood, a holy nation, a people belonging to God, that you may declare the praises of him who called you out of darkness into his wonderful light. (1 Peter 2:9)

When Michael Anderson entered his parent's bedroom, he noticed that nearly every inch of the bed was covered with suitcases. Each satchel, knapsack, and bag of every color imaginable was filled with everything from Sunday suits to shampoo and toothbrushes.

"My closet is almost bare," Michael greeted his mother, who was carefully counting out socks. She smiled as he continued. "I wish we could leave today! Why can't we just throw our stuff into the car and go?"

"I suppose it seems silly to you to plan our vacation in such detail."

Michael nodded. "I read your list of things to remember. Would it be so bad if we were to forget Tracy's hair ribbons, or

Dad's sunglasses, or Lindsay's curling iron? And what about your food list? You've planned every meal right down to the last apple and banana!"

Mrs. Anderson nodded and smiled. "Dad has his own list, too. He's planned just how much gas we'll need and how many times we can afford to eat in a restaurant along the way. He's made reservations in motels so we'll be sure to have a place to stay every night."

"You see," Mom continued, "if we'd hop into the car and just go, we might run out of money for gas, food, and motel rooms. If I forget to pack something we need, our vacation might not turn out to be very pleasant. A long trip takes plenty of planning, or we might never reach Grandma's at all!"

Just as the Anderson's long summer vacation trip needed to be planned carefully, so our lives also should be carefully planned. In the Bible, when Jacob appeared before the great Pharaoh of Egypt, he asked Jacob how old he was. Jacob replied, "The years of my pilgrimage (journey) are 130" (Genesis 47:9). You see, Jacob thought of his life as a long trip. He wanted Pharaoh to know that he was just passing through this earthly life and that he had his mind set on his heavenly home. God also wants us to look upon our lives as a trip or journey to heaven.

"Dad, how many more miles until we get to Grandma's?" Once the Anderson family was packed into the car and on the road, this question was asked constantly. In life, too, we never know how much time will go by before the last day of our journey comes, and we reach our destination.

The devil wants us to think we have plenty of time before we die—before our journey ends—to be sorry for our sins and believe in Jesus as our Savior. If the dust starts collecting on our Bibles, he tells us simply to brush it away. "You will have more time to read and study it tomorrow," he suggests. He wants to do everything possible to blind us to the fact that our journey through life is very short and that our journey could end this very night.

Let us keep reminding each other to plan for our final destination, our new life in heaven, by reading, hearing, and studying God's Word. As we do this, we become more certain that Jesus truly is our Savior and has freely forgiven us all of our sins. Use your Bible faithfully just as Mr. Anderson used his road map to guide his family along the highways on their journey to Grandma's. May we never forget that life is really just a trip to a heavenly destination and that the rest of our life, eternal life, begins there.

Prayer: Dear Jesus, please call me back when I start to stray away from your holy word. Remind me always that I am free of my sin through you alone. Amen.

The Right Kind Of Sorrow

Godly sorrow brings repentance that leads to salvation and leaves no regret, but worldly sorrow brings death. (2 Corinthians 7:10)

Lindsay Anderson eagerly looked through the mail to see if she had received any birthday cards. Sure enough, there at the bottom of the pile was a card for her. She frowned when she noticed the envelope had already been opened. The verse made her smile, but her grandmother's writing in the corner confused her. It read, "Five dollar gift enclosed." Lindsay searched through the envelope but found nothing.

"Maybe Grandma forgot to put it in," Mom comforted her daughter, when she learned about the missing money.

After supper Melissa and Michael settled down to play a game of checkers. As Michael stretched to jump his sister's checker, she spotted something strange and asked, "What's that green thing sticking out of your pocket?"

"Oh, nothing," lied Michael as he pushed the bill deeper into his jeans.

"*You* didn't take Lindsay's birthday money, did you?" Melissa asked accusingly.

Lindsay overheard the conversation. Coming over to the children's table, she just stared at her brother.

"Oh, this," Michael laughed. With sweaty hands he pulled the bill from his pocket. "I found this on the way home from school," he lied.

When Mom and Dad questioned him, Michael admitted he had taken Lindsay's money.

"You've stolen, Michael," Dad said sternly. "Then you lied to cover it up."

"I'm sorry," Michael confessed. He hung his head to hide the tears welling up in his eyes.

Mr. Anderson, seeing Michael's tears of shame, thought he had been punished enough. "I hope we'll be able to trust you again."

Michael nodded, but under his breath he muttered, "If only Melissa wouldn't always be so snoopy . . ."

How sorry do you think Michael really was? Oh, he was sorry—sorry he was *caught* taking Lindsay's money, but he wasn't sorry he took it. This is false sorrow. This is not the kind of sorrow God is looking for. When the words, I'm sorry, come from our lips, they should mean we are sad we hurt someone else. They should also mean we are sad we hurt Jesus by breaking his commandment. This is godly sorrow. It's the only kind which leads us to want Jesus' forgiveness and trusts that he will give it to us.

Remember, we should never take our sin lightly. Sometimes our parents must remind us that we did wrong in a way that pains us, as Michael's father finally had to.

When you sin, go to God quickly, confess all your wrongs, and be truly sorry you committed them. Be confident then that your true Father, for Jesus' sake, will never turn you away.

Prayer: Dear Jesus, help us to feel truly sorry for our sins. We hurt you when we do wrong. Thank you for forgiving all of our sins. Amen.

God Who Is The "Alls"

Oh, the depth of the riches of the wisdom and knowledge of God! How unsearchable his judgments, and his paths beyond tracing out! (Romans 11:33)

"Haven't you ever wondered how God could create this whole world out of nothing?" Melissa Anderson asked her twin brother.

Michael looked up from the magazine he was reading. "Maybe you should talk to Mom," he chuckled. "She's been known to create an entire meal out of practically nothing."

Melissa smiled. "Yes, yes, but even Mom has to start with *something*! God used only the power of his word to create the world out of nothing."

"Creation isn't the only mind-boggler," Michael agreed. "How could Jesus, the Son of God, come to earth as a little baby? How could God fit into the body of one so tiny? For that matter, how could God die on a cross and then come back to life?"

"Some of the Bible's teachings are very mysterious, aren't they?" asked Dad, as he stepped into the family room.

Melissa bent her head and nodded. "I want to be a true believer," she said, "but my poor brain can't seem to understand how creation or the resurrection of Jesus was possible."

"Trying to understand everything in the Bible raises many questions," Dad agreed, "and it is by faith we deal with every one of them." Mr. Anderson paused momentarily and then asked, "Remember last Friday when we went over to see Aunt Lucy's new baby?"

Melissa smiled. "Little Allison," she giggled. "I've never seen a baby so cute and so sweet!"

"Cute, sweet, and don't forget very tiny," Dad added. "Do you suppose little Allison understands how she manages to stay so well fed?"

Melissa shrugged. "She's only a baby, Daddy. She cries

when she's hungry. She's happy when she's fed. She doesn't have to think about it."

"Very true, but I wonder if she understands how hard her mother and father must work to earn the money to buy the milk. Does she realize how her mother must open a can or take it cold from the refrigerator and warm it in a bottle on the stove?"

"What about the cow?" Michael interrupted. "Does Allison understand how the farmer raises the cows to produce the milk to be sold in the store?"

Melissa rolled her eyes toward the ceiling. "All this talk is pretty silly!" she exclaimed. "You can't expect a baby to understand everything."

Dad chuckled. "That's just my point. Neither should we human beings think it's so odd if we can't understand all the mysteries of our all-powerful God. Compared to the Almighty, we are like little babies. The Bible even tells us that the wisdom of God is unsearchable. That means we won't be able to figure out everything about our God until he himself gives us the answers in heaven."

"Well, Carol Stickney claims she won't believe anything she can't understand," Melissa said.

"And if little Allison would have the same attitude about understanding milk production, or our money system, or the love of parents for their children, she'd starve to death."

Melissa nodded. "Allison just opens her little mouth and trusts that the milk will be there. It always is," she replied, matter-of-factly.

"In the same way, we should just open our hearts and trust in God's word, even though we can't fully understand how everything it tells us can be true."

"Should we stop studying the Bible if we can't figure out all these mysteries?" asked Melissa.

"Not at all!" Dad answered. "It is through God's word we can be sure we are saved by Jesus' blood on the cross. And in the middle of trouble and pain we can read God's promises and know that he is always watching over us and guarding us. We may not understand all the why's and how's, but by faith we accept them as the truth because God revealed them to us."

"And when you are puzzled, Melissa," Michael added, "do what I do. Remember the 'Alls' God is."

"The 'Alls'?" asked Melissa.

"Sure, just like we learned in Sunday School. God is all-powerful, all-knowing, all-present, all-loving; the 'Alls'."

"Maybe that will help Carol Stickney," Melissa smiled. "Nothing is impossible for a God who is the 'Alls'."

Prayer: Dear Jesus, I feel just like a little baby when I try to understand all your mysteries. Give me a strong faith to trust in the "Alls" that you are. I believe you are my Savior. Amen.

What A Friend We Have In Jesus

Be strong and courageous. Do not be terrified; do not be discouraged, for the LORD your God will be with you wherever you go. **(Joshua 1:9)**

Mrs. Anderson sat in the window seat beside her youngest daughter, who was gazing sadly at the twinkling stars that filled the sky. "Why did Dolly have to move?" Tracy asked. "It really spoiled our plans for first grade."

"I know it did," Mom comforted her. "Dolly's daddy was promoted by his company. They wanted him to move back East."

"But his new job took away my best friend. I never had a better friend than Dolly. She knew what I was thinking before I thought it. She liked to do the same things I did. I'll never find another Dolly."

"Dolly was special to all of us, Tracy, but did you know you still have a best friend? This one will never move away!"

"I do?" asked Tracy.

Mom nodded. "When you are lonely and sad, he'll make you feel better. You can trust in him when you are afraid and . . ."

"You said he, Mom. Is my best friend a boy?" Tracy asked, her eyes wide with surprise.

Mom smiled. "I'm talking about Jesus, Tracy."

"Oh," Tracy grinned back and chuckled softly. "Jesus is my friend, but I never thought of him in the same way I thought of Dolly. I mean, I do love him very much, but I can't hold hands with him. I wish I could feel close to him like I did to Dolly."

"Oh, but you can, Tracy. You can feel even closer to Jesus. He's an even better friend. Remember how Dolly used to pull your hair when she got mad at you? Remember how she knocked you down so she could be first in line at recess?"

Tracy frowned. "But Dolly didn't mean to do those things. Once in a while she lost her temper, but most of the time she was a very good friend."

Mom nodded. "Yes, she was, but I want you to see that no human friend is perfect. Friends are sinners. They can let you down. At times they can make you sad."

"Is Jesus a perfect friend?"

"Yes, he is," Mom said with a smile. "Jesus gave his life for us to prove he is the greatest friend of all. And when he ascended into heaven, he promised he would never leave us or forsake us. It's true, he doesn't hold hands with you as you walk to the store, but he's still with you. So whether you're in school, at home, or on the playground—in fact, no matter where you are—he's always there with you."

"Jesus would never move away," Tracy added.

Mom nodded. "He's with us always, even in our worst disappointments. We can turn to him when we feel very low, and he has promised to help us. Even if none of our pals or family seems to care about us, we know Jesus does. He wants to wipe away our tears. He wants us to cling to him for our happiness."

"Does he want to help me get through losing a really good friend?"

"He wants to fill the emptiness by supplying you with many new friends."

Tracy nodded. "But no matter how many friends he gives me, I'll always remember I have one truly perfect friend in Jesus."

Prayer: Dear Jesus, sometimes I feel so lonely, especially when I don't have a special friend to talk to. Forgive me for forgetting that you are my best and truest friend. Amen.

Wake Up! I Hear You Snoring!

Better is one day in your courts than a thousand elsewhere; I would rather be a doorkeeper in the house of my God than dwell in the tents of the wicked. **(Psalm 84:10)**

Michael tossed his baseball glove into the dirt and plunked himself down on the backyard swing. His twin sister came running across the lawn toward him, bubbling over with excitement.

"Hi, Michael," she greeted him. She pulled off his baseball cap and pushed it down low over her own head. "How was practice? Did you get a chance to talk to Tommy Sands? Did he say he'd come with us for Invitation Sunday at church?"

Michael shook his head sadly. "He's not coming," he answered softly. "He says church is just too boring."

"But he came last year," Melissa persisted.

"Last year the church picnic followed the service," Michael explained.

"Hmmm," Melissa nodded. "You didn't have anything to bribe him with this year. Is that it?"

Michael nodded in discouragement. "It's too bad. I guess he was more interested in the picnic part than in the church part. But how about you, Melissa? Do you sometimes think like Tommy does? Do you think church is boring, too?"

Melissa swallowed hard and looked away. "Well, once in a while I do get tired of sitting so still. The sermon is pretty long, especially in the summer when it's hot."

"Would you be happier not going then?" asked Michael.

"No, I wouldn't," Melissa answered. "But there was a time when I thought I was fooling everybody. I'd go to church and try to think of hundreds of things to make the time go faster. My excuse was always the same. I didn't think I would be able to understand what the pastor was saying anyway, so I didn't try. I figured church was mainly for grown-ups."

"What made you change your mind?"

"Well, one Sunday Dad gave me a really sharp poke. He noticed I was getting dizzy counting the dots on Mrs. Beasley's dress. He told me it would make the time go really fast if I'd listen instead."

Michael nodded and smiled. "I doubt whether Dad was that much interested in the time going faster. He just wanted you to pay attention to the sermon."

"I know. I caught on to that later. I also began to feel ashamed of myself. Here the pastor had spent a whole week preparing a sermon for a girl who was trying her hardest not to listen. I was acting as though he was speaking in a foreign language that I couldn't understand. Once I tried to listen, I found I could understand almost everything he was talking about."

How about you? Do you think church is boring? It is the devil who puts this idea into our heads in the first place. He gets the Melissa's to count polka dots or the Tommys to look forward only to the picnic after the service. How sad God must be to see how halfheartedly we worship him sometimes!

In our Bible reading the psalmist's heart is glad when he thinks about going to church. He is going there to worship God in a spirit of real joy. He is going there to worship the God of his salvation, the God who had created and redeemed him. He knows that at church God is present in a very special way. He is going there to praise God by singing hymns and psalms, to listen to God speak to him through his word, and to bring his offering to his Lord. He is going there to place all his problems and cares in the Lord's hands as he talks to the Lord in prayer.

Sometimes church may seem boring because we have lost sight of why we are going there in the first place and of all the grand things that happen there. Never forget! In church we talk to God, and he talks to us. In church we worship God and praise him.

When you come to think about it, worship is all we can give to God. After all, there is nothing God needs or lacks. And there is nothing that God wants except whole-hearted worship from his creatures.

True worship is a matter of the heart. It comes out of a thankful heart, a heart that is hungry to hear the word of God, a heart that is anxious to be filled with the grace and power of God. Can we do any less than this—worship him every Sunday, every day, every hour?

Prayer: Dear Jesus, sometimes I come to church with the attitude that I'm doing you a favor by worshipping. Forgive me when I worship so halfheartedly. Help me to see fully all the blessings you have given me in your word. Amen.

Why Work So Hard?

We hear that some among you are idle. They are not busy; they are busybodies. Such people we command and urge in the Lord Jesus Christ to settle down and earn the bread they eat. (2 Thessalonians 3:11,12)

Michael lay on his bed holding the TV listing up to the light. "Hey, Jason, there's a great movie on at eight. Come downstairs and watch it with me."

"I'd love to, Michael," Jason answered, "but I have two tests tomorrow. That's the trouble with Junior High: there seems to be a test every other day."

"We have tests in fourth grade, too," Michael answered with a yawn. "In fact, we have a Geography test tomorrow."

Jason looked up from the book he was studying. "Geography isn't exactly your best subject. How do you expect to watch a movie and still have time to prepare for a test?"

Michael shrugged. "I decided not to study."

"Oh, not studying will do wonders for your grade!" Jason scoffed. "Quit fooling around, Michael. Find your book!"

"I'm not fooling around, Jason. It makes no sense to study for a test I probably won't have to take."

"And why won't you have to take it?" asked his brother.

"Well, there happens to be a strong possibility the world will end tonight. Why should I waste my time studying for a test I might not have to take?"

Jason threw his head back, and the room rang with laughter. "Okay, okay, Michael, there is a good possibility the world could end tonight. On the other hand, it may be here in the morning the same as always, so hit those books!" he bellowed, springing onto the bed. With a bump and a tumble, both brothers rolled to the floor laughing and trying to catch their breath.

"If it'll make you happy, I'll study," Michael finally answered. "But if the world does end tonight, I'll blame you for making me miss a good movie!"

Jason shook his head and walked back to his desk. "It is good to be ready for the Lord's coming, Michael, but Jesus doesn't want us to be just sitting around and waiting. He wants us to tend to business."

"Remember the Thessalonian Christians in the Bible? Many of them were so excited about Jesus' return that they left their jobs and stopped working completely. Paul scolded them for being lazy and idle. He reminded them that God didn't want them wasting the precious time he had given them. So, as we wait for Jesus to come again, he wants to see us performing our ordinary tasks—going to school, taking tests, making meals, and caring for one another."

"But what if you thought you were going to die tonight? Wouldn't it be okay to take it easy today?" asked Michael.

"Well, think of Mr. Cooper from church. He could die any day because he has been seriously ill. But he knows that taking it easy won't help his disease go away. He still wants to help his family by putting food on the table and paying the bills. At work he also knows he'll have a chance to talk to other people who have problems. He'll be able to share the good news of what Jesus has done for him with those people," Jason answered. "You might say that Mr. Cooper is working while it is day."

Michael nodded and pulled his geography book down from the shelf. "If Jesus does come tonight, I'd rather he would find me doing what I'm supposed to be doing instead of goofing off."

Jason nodded as he settled back to his math book. "Believe me, Michael, whether it's Miss Kasten, or Jesus, who greets you tomorrow morning, you'll be ready!"

Prayer: Dear Jesus, I want to be ready for your coming at all times. Strengthen my faith that I always trust in you for the forgiveness of my sins. Help me do my work faithfully. I know this is one way I am able to thank you for dying on the cross for my sins. Amen.

Being A Real Follower Of Jesus

By this all men will know that you are my disciples, if you love one another. (John 13:35)

Mrs. Anderson was changing the sheets in the girl's room one Saturday morning. Melissa stood at one side of the bed and stretched the bottom sheet over the mattress. "How big is heaven?" she asked suddenly.

"No one knows exactly how big it is, Melissa, but God tells us he's preparing mansions for us there. So, we do know that there'll be plenty of room for everyone."

"Could it be so big that one person would never see another person there?" Melissa persisted.

"Oh, I think we'll be able to meet everyone," smiled Mrs. Anderson. "We'll certainly have plenty of time, since heaven lasts for all eternity. Why do you ask?"

"Well, Sara Blakely can't stand Jennifer Fremont. They are constantly fighting about something. Sara says heaven better be pretty big because she doesn't want to bump into Jennifer there!"

Mrs. Anderson nodded sadly. "It's sad that people often have such a hard time forgiving one another. But it's saddest of all when this happens between two Christians."

"I know Sara and Jennifer both believe in Jesus as their Savior," answered Melissa. "Will God keep them apart in heaven so they won't fight?"

"What do you think?" asked Mom. "Do you think there could be two people in heaven who still dislike each other?"

"I don't think so," answered Melissa. "Heaven is a happy place. No one will ever be sad or angry there!"

Mrs. Anderson nodded thoughtfully. "In the Bible, Jesus says we prove we are his disciples, or believers, by loving each other. So, if two people hate each other, they have to ask themselves whether they really love Jesus."

You may know of two people who fight constantly with one

another. Perhaps their fighting isn't even done out in the open. Rather they may walk around holding their bitter feelings toward one another inside.

Jesus doesn't want this to go on. He suffered and died that, believing in him, we might have forgiveness for our sins. Having been forgiven by him, we, in turn, are to forgive each other. So, out of love for God, let us forgive each other, love each other, and become friends again. With Jesus' help we can forgive, as he forgave us, and love, even as he loved us.

Prayer: Dear Jesus, please forgive me when I hold a grudge. Help me to make up with those people with whom I've had fights or disagreements. Please keep my place in heaven open. I'm sorry for all my sins! Amen.

The Lesson Of The Sunflower

I am the light of the world. Whoever follows me will never walk in darkness, but will have the light of life. (John 8:12)

Rows and rows of sunflowers spread across the open fields as the Andersons drove along the Interstate, coming home from their visit with Grandma and Grandpa.

Tracy, the youngest Anderson, stared curiously at the sunflowers. "This is really strange," she exclaimed. "When we drove this road Monday, I was sure those sunflowers were facing the other way. How did the farmer get them to turn their heads this way?"

Jason tousled the hair of his younger sister. "It wasn't the farmer, Tracy; it was the sun. The sunflower turns to face the sun, wherever it is. On Monday morning, when we came through here, the sun was just rising in the east. So the sunflowers pointed toward the east. It's almost suppertime now, and the sun is in the west, so the flowers are facing this way!"

Mr. Anderson nodded and smiled. "There is a wonderful picture for every Christian in what the sunflower plant does. The sunflower reminds us of how we should always keep our eyes focused on a different Son."

"Oh, I get it, not s-u-n, but S-O-N. We should always keep our eyes focused on Jesus. Pretty sharp, Dad," Lindsay smiled. "I have a friend in school, Misty Lee Simpson, who should hear this. I'm afraid her eyes have gotten off the S-O-N in just one short year."

"Wasn't Misty in your Confirmation class?" Mom asked.

"Yes," Lindsay replied, "but I'm afraid our classes and church don't mean much to her any more. She wanted to be popular. She wanted to belong to the 'in crowd,' to be part of a certain group of kids in town. To be accepted, she felt she had to smoke pot and use bad language and skip class constantly. Well, last week she was suspended from school. That group of kids really turned her head."

"The only way for any of us to keep from falling into the same kind of trap is to keep our eyes focused on Jesus. We have to listen to him as he speaks to us in his word. Otherwise, drugs and the desire to be popular can easily turn teenagers away from their Savior. Satan tempts and traps older people by using fancy homes, or new cars, or high-paying jobs as bait," Mom explained.

"Now, some of these things are wonderful blessings from God. But Satan likes to try and convince us these things are more exciting, more worthwhile than what Jesus has to offer us. Satan tries to make us think we don't need Jesus. He tries to convince us that it's these earthly things that can make us happy," Dad said.

"But only Jesus can save us," Tracy responded. "It's so obvious!"

"That is why, in order to be the best sunflowers of all, we need a childlike faith which trusts Jesus no matter what. When we have that sort of faith, the devil has a very hard time turning our heads away from the Lord," Mom explained.

May we never get to the point where we feel that we don't have to study God's word daily. Through it we are able to see our sin and realize we are lost without our Savior. Through it we learn of how we have been forgiven. As the lesson of the sunflower teaches, let us never take a single step without keeping our eyes focused on God's one and only S-O-N!

Prayer: Dear Jesus, the world is so dark with sin all around us. Everywhere I turn there are temptations. Keep my faith strong and my eyes focused upon you and your cross. You are the true and eternal light of my life. Amen.

Tomorrow May Be Too Late

Therefore keep watch, because you do not know the day or the hour. (Matthew 25:13)

"Forty-five dollars and ninety cents!" Michael Anderson declared triumphantly. "Give me another month and I'll have enough for a scooter of my very own!"

"Why wait a month?" asked Melissa. "You have enough already!"

"No, the scooter I was looking at costs nearly sixty dollars. Even with my allowance and doing odd jobs, I'll have to wait at least three more weeks."

"Not if you go tonight," Melissa explained quickly. "Swifts Department Store is having a 25%-off sale. Every item is on sale, including scooters."

The twins raced in to tell the entire story to Dad. They waited expectantly for his reply. "But, kids, the store closes at nine. We would hardly have enough time to get there tonight.

We'll go tomorrow instead." To his surprise the children began to talk even faster and more excitedly than before.

Dad laid the paper in his lap. "Are you telling me that if we don't go tonight, you can't get the 25% off? Well, then let's go. Grab your jackets and jump into the car! Even the sports page will have to wait tonight."

Mr. Anderson sped through the darkness so that Michael could purchase the shiny new scooter. There was no time to waste; tomorrow would be too late.

Yes, the times are urgent. We don't know when Christ will return to the earth. We have to be ready at all times.

Remember the parable Jesus told about the ten young women who were invited to the wedding? All of them carried oil in their lamps, but only five of them carried enough oil to last all night. The bridegroom in the story was Jesus. The long night represented life here on earth, and the oil represented faith. The five wise women knew they must keep hearing and studying God's word so their faith would not flicker and go out.

Early in the morning when the bridegroom, Jesus, appeared, the faith of these five wise women burned brightly, but the foolish women had let their oil of faith run out. They hadn't had time for Christ and his word. Now they could not enter heaven with the believing women. Now, it was too late.

As Michael closed his eyes to sleep, he knew his shiny scooter was tucked safely in the garage. Like Michael, we, too, would probably rush out to buy a toy on sale even though we know that we might grow tired of it very quickly.

With even more urgency, though, let us run to our Savior's cross, daily confessing our sins and trusting in his forgiveness. Let us use the oil of faith which the Holy Spirit has lit in our hearts to live for Christ, bringing others to him as well. Tomorrow may be too late.

Prayer: Dear Jesus, forgive me for not running to your word as quickly as I'd run for a sale. Give me a strong faith to be ready whenever you may come. Amen.

Only What's Best For Me

If you, then, though you are evil, know how to give good gifts to your children, how much more will your Father in heaven give good gifts to those who ask him! **(Matthew 7:11)**

After another long coughing spasm, Melissa rested her head heavily on the couch pillow. She could hear her mother rummaging through the kitchen cabinets in search of the cough medicine.

"I wish I wouldn't have to take that awful medicine!" Melissa croaked, putting her hand to her sore throat.

Suddenly, the sound of shattered glass echoed from the kitchen. "Oh, no," Mom cried. "It broke. And not one drop is left!"

"Oh, dear" Melissa groaned wearily. "I can't stop coughing without my medicine."

"But just a moment ago you wished you didn't have to take it," Lindsay argued.

Melissa sighed. "I know I did, but it's only because I can't stand the taste. I really didn't mean what I said. Mom knows I need my awful-tasting medicine and I do, too!"

Do you remember a time when you asked your parents for something you really wanted, but you didn't get it? Perhaps you had your eye on a certain toy or bag of candy, but Mom and Dad didn't give in to your wishes.

Why? The answer is an easy one, though it might be hard for us to accept. Parents who love their children want only what is good for them. They know, for example, that too much candy spoils teeth. They know too many toys may spoil their children. So, in spite of tantrums and tears, loving parents won't give in to their children when they know they will be harmed by what they want. Loving parents only give gifts that are for their children's good.

If this is true about sinful parents, it is doubly true about

God. Only God knows, not only exactly what we want, but also what we truly need. God may choose not to make us as good looking as we'd like to be. He can see how such blessings might turn us into walking snobs, only caring for ourselves. God may not give us as many friends or as much money as we'd like to have. There might be the danger that we would begin to think we didn't need him as much. Of course, good looks, smarts, many friends, and money aren't bad in themselves, but only God knows how many material and bodily blessings it would take to pull us away from loving him above all things.

Out of love for us, God doesn't give us everything we want, but he does promise to give us everything we need. He promises to keep on loving us and to care for our bodily needs. He promises to bring his word to us through faithful pastors. He promises us the forgiveness of sins through Jesus' death on the cross. He especially promises to give us believers eternal life in heaven.

What a wonderful gift of love he has given us—to be able to pray for anything we need or want, knowing he will never give us anything which will hurt us. As Melissa says about her mother and father, may we also say about our God: He knows what's best for me.

Prayer: Dear Jesus, sometimes what is best for me is not always so easy for me to accept. Give me the strength to trust in you, to know that all things you allow to happen are done to keep my faith in you secure. Amen.

Looking For Trouble?

No one who is born of God will continue to sin, because God's seed remains in him; he cannot go on sinning, because he has been born of God. **(1 John 3:9)**

"The entire house is ours while your parents are away!" cried Mona. "What kind of trouble can we get ourselves into first?"

"Trouble?" Melissa asked, giving her cousin a suspicious look. She held up a list of duties her mother had left. "Make beds, dust, vacuum, do dishes, empty garbage. Nope! Trouble isn't even listed," she giggled, grabbing the sheets and taking the steps to her bedroom two by two.

"Forget the beds!" Mona cried, catching up with her cousin. "Your mom will never know the beds haven't been changed."

Melissa frowned. "No, but I'll know. I like sleeping in a fresh bed!"

"C'mon, Melissa, forget the boring duty list. Let's get busy doing something really fun." Mona spotted Lindsay's diary near her bed. "How about reading your sister's diary? We can find out all about her boyfriends. I know how to pick a lock."

Melissa shook her head.

"Then, how about putting on your mother's makeup or telephoning Alaska?"

"Mona! I don't even know anyone in Alaska! You sure do have your mind set on getting into mischief."

"Of course," Mona replied flippantly. "What good is being left home alone if you can't get away with something?"

Melissa stared at her cousin. "Dad puts it another way. He says when you are left alone, instead of thinking of all the wrong you can do, think of ways you can prove you are God's child, and do them!"

Are you God's child? Since you have been baptized, you belong to God. When the pastor poured the water on you and spoke God's word, the Holy Spirit began to work faith in your heart, faith that believes Jesus is your Savior, faith that makes you a child of God.

In 1 John 3:9, God tells us that no one who is born of God will continue to sin. Yet when the day is over, we can think of many, many ways in which we have sinned. Does this mean we should be rebaptized again to become God's child? No! Not at all. Our baptism is good for all time, but we can renew our baptism every day simply by telling God we are truly sorry for our sins and asking his forgiveness.

There are some sins which catch us off guard. There are other sins which we plan just as Mona did. The sins we plan are especially dangerous for our soul, because we are purposely going against God.

The way we live our lives proves whose child we want to be. Let us feel sorry for all of our sins and, with God's help, may we never go looking for trouble. Instead, let us find true happiness in living as God's children.

Prayer: Dear Jesus, there have been times when I've looked for trouble as if I enjoy sinning against you. Forgive me for not taking to heart your suffering and death. Give me the power to say no to any sin, planned or unplanned. Amen.

Comfort, Comfort

Comfort, comfort my people, says your God. Speak tenderly to Jerusalem, and proclaim to her that her hard service has been completed, that her sin has been paid for, that she has received from the LORD's hand double for all her sins. (Isaiah 40:1,2)

Tenderly, Mom picked up her youngest child and rushed her into the house. Gently, she laid her on the serving counter. Quickly she moistened several paper towels and carefully dabbed each wound caused by the merciless sidewalk. Tracy's hysterical screams finally subsided into quiet sobs.

Jason watched from the kitchen table, a silent observer of the entire scene. "I don't get it, Mom," he said, watching his bandaged sister raise herself to sit. "Is this or is this not the same little girl who pestered you for weeks to try Lindsay's new skateboard? And, are you or are you not the mother who explained dozens of times how dangerous skateboards can be for a girl her age?"

Mom wiped away Tracy's last tear. "Yes, we're guilty on all counts, Jason, but what are you getting at?" asked Mom.

"Well, how can you be so gentle and forgiving after Tracy deliberately disobeyed you?"

"Yes, I know," Mom spoke solemnly. "A spanking really was in order."

"Well," Jason fumbled, "I know you couldn't have punished her as she lay bleeding on the sidewalk, but you are almost overly gentle with her now. She really got what she deserved, you know."

Mom smiled. "Yes, but isn't that the way it is with all of us? Remember when you were small and fell out of the tree in the back yard? Dad had specifically told you not to climb it. Yet, what did he do when you fell?"

"He picked me up, checked for any broken bones, and held me really close. I was so frightened, but he kept telling me I was okay."

"He didn't treat you as you deserved, either," Lindsay added. "It's just like the Israelites in the Bible. Remember how they often fell away from God and worshiped idols even though they had been warned many times before?"

"God had to jar the Israelites to their senses to make them feel sorry for their sins. This was one of the reasons God let them be taken captive by the Babylonians. He wanted them to repent and turn again to him as their God."

"Their captivity was kind of like falling off a skateboard," Tracy spoke up. "It taught them a lesson and put them on the right track again."

Mom nodded. "Even when they were taken away into captivity, God didn't forget about them. They were to recall the words of the prophet Isaiah. He promised their sins would be paid back, not as they deserved, but by a double portion of God's goodness."

"Was his double portion Jesus?" asked Jason.

"Yes, instead of casting them away, he gave them a Savior," Mom finished. "You see, Jason, God always has treated us with much kindness. That is why we don't want to be too harsh with someone who . . ."

"Has just fallen off a skateboard she wasn't supposed to be riding," Tracy finished.

"Or with someone who fell out of a tree he wasn't supposed to be climbing," Jason said. He rumpled his sister's hair. "If you promise to stay off skateboards until you are eight and wear protective padding, I'll give you a piggy-back ride."

Tracy's eyes brightened as she sniffled her last. She grabbed her brother's neck as he carefully held her bandaged legs. "I promise," she giggled happily.

Prayer: Dear Jesus, thank you for comforting me with the forgiveness of my sins. Help me to show kindness instead of harshness when I deal with others. Amen.

Love Your Enemies

But love your enemies, do good to them, and lend to them without expecting to get anything back. Then your reward will be great, and you will be sons of the Most High, because he is kind to the ungrateful and wicked. (Luke 6:35)

"You'll have apple juice pouring out of your hand if you squeeze it any tighter," Michael warned his sister.

Melissa stared at the crushed apple. "I didn't mean to take it out on my lunch," she replied. "I just wish I could squeeze some human feelings into Laurie Willis. She doesn't care whom she hurts. She told me softball tryouts were next week instead of yesterday. She was afraid I'd beat her out for the second base position. Now I don't know if I'll be able to try out at all."

"Don't worry, Melissa, some of the guys in our class heard all about it and decided to teach Laurie a lesson."

"What kind of a lesson?" Melissa asked guardedly.

"Oh, we just mixed up a few days on the calendar like she did. She thinks Nerd Day is today instead of next week. Isn't that great?"

Melissa's eyes grew large. "Do you mean Laurie thinks today is the day we are supposed to dress really crazy?"

"Yeah, won't this be hilarious? Bobby Owens loaned her a curly wig and a mismatched outfit from his sister. Laurie will really be embarrassed when she realizes no one else dressed up. Your enemy is going to be paid back and then some."

"My enemy?" The words echoed back and forth in Melissa's head. Was Laurie Willis really her enemy? They had been talking about enemies in Sunday School.

During Jesus' day, the Samaritans and the Jews were terrible enemies. The Jews despised the Samaritans because they had married their unbelieving neighbors who worshiped idols instead of the true God. The Samaritans worshiped these heathen gods even while they were worshiping the Lord. God didn't approve of this, but the Jews had no right to hate and despise them. To show them that they should love their neighbors as themselves, Jesus told the story of the Good Samaritan.

One day a Samaritan was traveling along the road to Jerusalem. He spotted a man lying in the road, bleeding and half-dead. What was the Samaritan to do? Here was his chance to get back at those Jewish people who despised him so. He could easily have ignored the man's cries for help. Instead, he jumped down from his donkey and gave him first aid on the spot. He cleaned the man's wounds and gave him food. Then he took him to an inn where he could be cared for.

He paid the innkeeper enough money to cover his expenses for the time it would take the wounded man to recover.

Melissa's forehead knotted into a frown. How could the good Samaritan be so kind, even to pay for the man's room? This Samaritan loved God who had first loved him. His heart, in turn, was filled with love for his fellowman. This is what prompted him into action when he saw the wounded man. He did not worry whether the same robbers might attack him. He did not consider how much time and work and money it would cost him. He did not stop to think how this "enemy" might have treated him if he had been the one who had been attacked and beaten. His one concern was to help this man. Everything he did was prompted by the love in his heart.

Five minutes before the bell would ring, Melissa and Michael entered the school building. As Melissa hung up her coat, she heard a few boys mention Laurie's name. It seemed her rival was in the restroom changing into her clothes for Nerd Day.

Michael entered the classroom a few minutes later, patiently waiting for his twin to join him. Finally at the sound of the bell, Melissa did enter. But what was this? Laurie was following directly behind, wearing perfectly normal clothes. Where was the black wig? Where was the mismatched clothing?

As Melissa slipped into her seat, Michael nudged her shoulder. "I am sorry, Melissa. Someone must have tipped Laurie off!"

"Yes, someone must have," Melissa grinned at her brother.

"You? You told her it wasn't Nerd Day? But why? You could have really gotten even with her."

"Yes, and all I'd have accomplished is gaining a worse enemy than I had before. Instead of revenge, I got something even better — a new friend."

Prayer: Dear Jesus, please help me to swallow my pride and forgive others when they treat me badly. Help me to remember how kind you were to me to forgive all my sins on the cross. Amen.

Inside Courage

Be on your guard; stand firm in the faith; be men of courage; be strong. **(1 Corinthians 16:13)**

Michael Anderson sat on his bed with his back to the open window. Every few minutes he turned to look at the nest of tiny baby robins snuggled in among the leafy branches. Suddenly he rose from his bed and reached for a BB gun hidden in the clothes closet. He found the three tender babies in the gun's sight, took careful aim and . . .

"Michael!" called a voice from the doorway. "What do you think you are doing?" Jason bellowed, whisking the gun from his brother's hand. "Were you really going to blow away those poor, defenseless birds? Where did you get this gun anyway?" Jason demanded.

Michael lowered his head. "B.J. Walker gave it to me."

"B.J.? But he goes to *my* school. Why are you running around with him?"

"I'm friends with his brother. We wanted to get into B.J.'s gang. He said that first we had to prove we were very, very brave."

"Do you really think shooting BB's into little birds shows courage? Don't you care about anything?"

Michael blinked fast. "I do care about those babies," he sniffed. "I watched them hatch from their eggs. I watched their mother bring them food. B.J. heard me talking about them and decided I cared too much. He said I had to kill them, or I was just too soft to be in his gang."

"There's nothing soft or weak about caring for little birds or anyone else who is helpless. Being cruel doesn't turn a boy into a man."

"Then, what does turn a boy into a man?" asked Michael. "Shouldn't a guy be strong?"

"Yes, very strong," Jason answered, but big muscles don't make the whole man. Men, and women too, must be strong on the inside as well as the outside. Anyone can act tough, but a real man stands up for what is right. He defends those he loves. He's not afraid to say what he thinks and believes. If you really want to be a man, look at the kind of man Jesus was."

Michael thought for a moment. "Jesus must have been strong in his body; he was a carpenter."

Jason nodded, "Yeah, the Bible says Jesus kept growing in physical size and in favor with God and man. While he had a strong body, the fact that he was well-liked and respected by those who knew him showed he had many inside strengths, too. The people among whom he grew up approved of the godly life he lived and respected him for it. When he grew older, he had the courage to preach to every kind of sinner, even though the church leaders didn't approve."

"But the most courageous thing Jesus ever did was to suffer and die on the cross for our sins. It took inside courage to pray for the enemies who were mocking him and for the soldiers who had crucified him and for all the others who had caused him so much pain. By staying up on the cross, feeling the nails rip into his skin, letting his bones be pulled out of joint, bearing up under leg cramps as he stretched for each breath, and finally dying, he showed the most enormous courage and strength. For, this was done to pay for people's sins," Jason said.

"Only love could have made him go through so much pain for us," Michael said, easing the gun out of his brother's hand. "I think I know a little more about what it takes to be a man. I'm ready to give B.J. his gun back."

"Do you want me to come and do some of the explaining for you?" asked Jason.

"Naw, I'll go myself," Michael answered. "I may have flunked B.J.'s test of courage, but now it's time to pass a different test of *inside* courage!"

Prayer: Dear Jesus, so many kids think it's courageous to be cruel. Help me to show my love for you by doing what is right. Forgive me when I fail. Amen.

131

Like A Soft Kitty

Be self-controlled and alert. Your enemy the devil prowls around like a roaring lion looking for someone to devour. **(1 Peter 5:8)**

Jason stumbled wearily into the kitchen. His hair and clothing were covered with ashes. Even his breath tasted of ashes and smoke. As he sipped the icy milk slowly, he felt the loving pressure of his mother's hand on his shoulder.

"When we told you it was okay to spend the night at Joe's, we never dreamed his house would catch fire. You could have been swept out of our lives forever."

Jason clasped his mother's hand. "I'm all right, Mom, really. It's Joe's sister I'm concerned about. She has second degree burns on her right hand because she didn't wake up as quickly as the rest of us."

"The smoke from the fire probably kept her from realizing what was happening," Dad explained. "Smoke can be overpowering."

"It was smoke, all right, which kept her from waking up, but I'm afraid it wasn't just the smoke from the fire."

"What other smoke was there?" asked little Tracy.

"It was the smoke from the marijuana cigarettes she had smoked right before going to bed. Joe thinks it's the pot which made her sleep so heavily. Joe says she's been experimenting with different kinds of illegal drugs at parties. I just hope the fire shakes her up enough so she wants to quit."

"Why does Joe's sister want to take drugs and sleep so heavily anyway?" asked Tracy. "Everyone knows playing is the most fun!"

"Some people think that drugs help to take away their problems. Getting drunk on alcohol or high on drugs sometimes makes a person forget about his troubles for the moment, so many people foolishly tamper with them," Dad explained.

"Exactly! Using illegal drugs or getting drunk is never smart. God wants us wide awake in life. He doesn't want us to hide behind drugs when we are troubled or afraid or lonely. He wants us to take all of our troubles to him in prayer," Mom answered.

"With all the classes we've had in school on drugs, I can hardly believe Joe's sister didn't realize how dangerous they are," Lindsay complained.

"I'm sure she knew the *facts* about drugs, but she probably felt she had power to stop using them whenever she wanted to." Mom said.

"Then, she must have forgotten how easily the body gets used to drugs and alcohol and starts to depend on them, and how using them becomes a habit that's very difficult to break. After taking them for even a short time, it gets to the point where a person's mind wants to say no, but the body is still saying yes. The body knows it'll get sick if it can't get the drugs it craves," Lindsay explained.

"Remember the passage we learned awhile ago?" asked Dad. "It is found in 1 Peter 5:8. 'Be self-controlled and alert. Your enemy the devil prowls around like a roaring lion looking for someone to devour.' One of the ways the devil does his prowling is through the use of illegal drugs."

"The devil doesn't want us to be sober or alert to all the dangers out there. He doesn't want us to be ready for our

Lord to come. Through drugs he blinds us to the seriousness of our sins. To prevent us from turning to our Lord Jesus for forgiveness and for help with our troubles, he hands us a bottle of pills and tells us to pretend our troubles don't exist," Mom explained.

"He makes drugs appear so appealing—as safe and lovable as a soft kitty sitting in our lap. But when we start taking drugs, the soft kitty turns into a ferocious lion, making us a prisoner of drugs!" Dad exclaimed.

"When I get big, I'm never going to fool with illegal drugs," Tracy announced to the family.

"This, too, we're not able to do on our own, Tracy. Only with God's help will any of us be able to say no to drugs or any kind of temptation which tries to pull us away from our Savior," Mom answered.

Prayer: Dear Jesus, give me the courage to say no to illegal drugs. Help me never to use alcohol in the wrong way. Give me the strength to fight against the temptations of Satan. Amen.

Better Half

Husbands, love your wives, just as Christ loved the church and gave himself up for her. (Ephesians 5:25)

Michael licked his lips as he took the long knife and carefully sliced the last piece of chocolate cake in half. With a gentle touch he lifted one half onto a clean plate. He waited patiently, wondering which piece his twin sister would pick.

"You know that not all halves are equal, don't you?" asked Melissa.

"Sure," replied Michael, "that's why Mom says one of us should cut, and the other gets the first pick. She knows that the one who cuts will then be fair."

Melissa studied the two pieces. "But if halves are supposed to be equal, why are Mom and Dad always talking about their better half? How can an equal half be better?"

Michael's eyes twinkled merrily. "They aren't talking about two pieces of cake, Melissa. Mom and Dad are talking about themselves. Married, they make a whole. They're united, but separate they each think of the other person as better than they are."

"That is a good way of thinking," Melissa replied. She took her fingers and crossed the very tips. "If Mom thinks Dad is better and Dad thinks Mom is better, they are really united."

"Sure," Michael replied, still studying the pieces of cake. It'll be harder for anything to split them apart."

"Tommy Sands' parents are getting a divorce," Melissa said suddenly. "Do you think his mom and dad stopped thinking of each other as better than each other?"

Michael nodded solemnly. He held up his fingers just as his sister had done, but he curled the tips. "Now try to pull my hands apart, Missy."

Melissa placed her hands over her brother's. "You are too strong, Michael. I can't do it."

Michael nodded. "I curled them to show how each man and wife have to have something else besides their own love to hold them together. The reason they think of each other as better is not only because of their love for each other, but also because of the faith inside of them."

"Which shows their love for Jesus," Melissa added.

"Dad says Jesus doesn't want marriages to split apart. If you care about what Jesus wants, you'll work harder to hold your marriage together."

"Jesus was never married himself," Melissa replied thoughtfully, "but he was always trying to treat people as if they were better than he. Remember how he washed his disciples' feet."

"He even ate with people who didn't have a very good reputation."

"And even cast devils out of those possessed by them," Melissa added. "While he did those things to save us sinners, do you suppose he was also trying to show us how to treat each other better than ourselves, even if we *aren't* married?" With a little shove she pushed one of the pieces toward her brother.

"Yes, I think Jesus was saying exactly that," Michael answered, frowning at the piece of cake his sister had given to him. "Melissa, I tried to slice them equally, but I'm afraid this still is the bigger piece. You have every right to it."

"I suppose I do," Melissa agreed, "but chocolate cake looks better on you than it does on me. I don't want people telling us apart by which one is chubbier," she grinned.

With a smile Michael lifted a large forkful of frosting and cake to his lips. "Here's to my better twin," he winked.

Prayer: Dear Jesus, it'll be quite a few years before I am married. Please get me ready for that time by teaching me to treat others better than myself. Thank you for treating me so kindly by forgiving my sins. Amen.

It's Not Fair

Now if we are children, then we are heirs—heirs of God and co-heirs with Christ, if indeed we share in his sufferings in order that we may also share in his glory. **(Romans 8:17)**

"It's just not fair!" yelled Jason, throwing his soccer ball at the closet door. He stared hatefully at the cast on his broken ankle, which had kept him in bed for the past two days. "Out of soccer for the rest of the season" he fumed. "It's just not fair!"

Suddenly a quiet knock sounded on his bedroom door. "Quit bothering me! Can't you see I'm trying to sleep?" he screamed in frustration.

The gray head of an elderly lady peered from around the corner. "I am sorry, Jason. I'll come back later after your nap."

"No, no, Mrs. Sage. Please come in," Jason answered, embarrassed over the tone of voice he had used with this family friend. "I thought you were Michael coming to pester me again."

"No, just old Mrs. Sage come to pay you a visit." She hobbled over to a chair and fell heavily into it. "I am sorry to hear about your injury, Jason. I know how disappointed you must be to sit out the rest of the soccer season."

A bright color filled Jason's cheeks. "What I am suffering is nothing compared to the pain you must have felt when your two kneecaps were shattered in the car accident."

"I guess we both have a share in pain," Mrs. Sage smiled. "Of course, bodily pain is nothing compared to losing Charlie and the kids."

Jason nodded. Charlie had been her husband for fifty years. He and their three small great-grandchildren had all been killed in that car accident. "So many sad things have happened to you, but here you are trying to cheer me up. How can you be so happy?"

"Oh, I had my bitter moments, too," Mrs. Sage confessed. "It was when I was sorting out some old photo albums that my feelings changed."

"How could old pictures make you feel happy again?"

"Well, they gave me a chance to examine my life. It had been a happy life, you know, not much pain and not a whole lot of trouble."

"And then God pulled the bottom out on all that happiness," Jason complained. "He took Charlie, he took the kids, and he left you crippled. It just isn't . . ."

"Fair?" Mrs. Sage asked. "It wasn't fair either for God to show me so much happiness all the years before the accident. As a sinner, I didn't deserve that either."

"I never looked at it that way," Jason confessed.

"Who does? We take all the good things for granted, as if God owed us a life of happiness. When I examined my life, I could hardly find one tiny cross I had been given to bear."

"Until now," Jason said softly.

Mrs. Sage nodded. "I decided I either could live out the rest of my life in bitterness and anger, blaming God and everyone else for my trouble, or I could bear it all, remembering how much Jesus suffered to pay for my sins."

Jason stared at his useless ankle. "It wasn't fair that Jesus had to suffer for what we did wrong. But he sure passed the test of love for us when he died on the cross. Do you think he could be using my broken ankle as a small test of my love for him?"

"Most certainly," Mrs. Sage replied, struggling to stand. "And remember, the way you stand up under pain can be an encouragement for others. Every test God sends us is a sample of his love, even the most horrible pain and sorrow."

"It is?" asked Jason.

"Yes, because through each trouble God teaches us to trust in and rely on *him* instead of our own strengths and abilities. He's *upping* your faith, Jason. There's only one word to describe that — LOVE!" With a wave and a half dozen hobbles, Mrs. Sage was gone. A smile spread over Jason's face. It was the first hint of happiness in two whole days. He picked up his guitar and began to strum softly.

Prayer: Dear Jesus, it's so easy to accept your blessings, but I need help accepting the troubles you test me with. Help me to see how you turn all problems into good for me. Thank you, Lord. Amen.

Death Is Like A Swinging Door

The sting of death is sin, and the power of sin is the law. But thanks be to God! He gives us the victory through our Lord Jesus Christ. **(1 Corinthians 15:56,57)**

Andrew knocked several times at the back door of the Anderson's house. Seeing the door was open a crack, he stepped inside. "Tracy! Tracy! Are you home? Can you play?" Still hearing no reply, he cautiously stepped down the hallway, continuing to call his classmate's name.

At the door of the living room he stopped. Tracy lay motionless on the rug of the living room floor. Her head drooped heavily to one side. Andrew stepped closer. Her eyelids lay perfectly still; her mouth was a relaxed line across her face. Was she sleeping? Andrew watched to see if her chest raised with her breathing. It too lay so still. Could Tracy be . . ."

"Oh, hi, Andrew!" Tracy called, popping upright, nearly knocking poor Andrew backward. "Want to play?"

"Tracy!" he exclaimed. "I thought you were dead the way you were lying there."

"How could I be dead?" she giggled. "We walked home from school only half an hour ago. I was just playing dead, the way Miss Price told us some animals do when they are afraid another animal might attack them. I'm very good at it. Want to try?"

"Nothing doing," Andrew replied firmly. "Playing dead reminds me too much of being dead. I don't even want to think about death!"

"Mom says we all have to face death. Even five-year-olds die."

"Maybe so, but I'm happier not thinking about it. Who wants to be a scary skeleton in a box? Who wants to be put underground? They buried my Grandma in the middle of winter, never caring that she probably froze to death."

"Andrew, your grandma was dead already," Tracy reminded him. "She couldn't feel the cold. The living part of her, you know, the soul, passed out of her body when she died."

"Then, that's the scary part. Who wants to be flying around the world like a ghost no one can see?"

"Andrew, you are all mixed up. God says in the Bible there are only two places the soul can go when the body dies. Either a person goes to heaven or to hell."

"See, Tracy, dying is scary. What if God puts me into hell?"

"If you believe Jesus has forgiven all the bad you have done, you never have to be afraid of going to hell. Hell is used for punishing sin. Because Jesus took away your sins, there is really nothing to punish you for."

"What if Jesus changes his mind about saving me?"

"He can't, Andrew. The saving part really has been done already. You just believe what Jesus has done for you. You receive it as a gift. You see, Andrew, the one who paid for your sins wasn't just a man. He is God, too. Jesus not only died for you, but he is also the one who will wake you up on the last day."

"Tracy, you make death sound so easy. I wonder why so many people are afraid of it."

"It could be because many people try to face death alone, without Jesus. Mom says death is like a swinging door. If you die believing in Jesus, the door swings open to heaven. If you die without believing, the door swings open to hell."

Andrew nodded thoughtfully. "The important thing is to die

believing. Then I won't be afraid which way the door is swinging."

"With Jesus it can only swing open one way—to heaven!" Tracy exclaimed with a smile.

Prayer: Dear Jesus, death sometimes brings fear to my heart. Remind me at all times how I am forgiven for your sake. When I die, carry me safely through death's door to your heavenly home. Amen.

I Wish I Was . . .

Delight yourself in the LORD and he will give you the desires of your heart. (Psalm 37:4)

Melissa leaned over the dresser and examined her face carefully in the mirror. She pushed her nose up and then down. Lindsay caught a glimpse of her sister's strange actions. "Doing your nose exercises?" she chuckled softly.

Melissa smiled into the mirror. "No, I was just wishing my nose was prettier—you know, turned up on the end like Laurie Willis' nose. Melissa sighed and grabbed a clump of her dark blonde hair. "If only my hair were lighter, too."

"Like Laurie's?" asked Lindsay.

Melissa nodded and sighed again. "I wish we could trade bodies too. I don't think I've lost all my baby fat yet."

Lindsay chuckled softly. "How about Laurie's heart? Do you want her insides, too?"

Melissa laughed and walked over to Lindsay's bed and sat down. "I suppose I'm talking silly. But why did God give some people all the good looks and leave others out in the cold?"

"I don't think God exactly left you out in the cold, Melissa. Although, there is no denying it. Laurie Willis is beautiful. She could be a model."

"See?" Melissa answered defiantly.

"All I see is that God gave Laurie an extra blessing of beauty. On the other hand, would you really give up all of your blessings to actually *be* Laurie?"

"I'd be very popular. I'd get A's all the time. I'd own my own ten-speed, not to mention a new outfit to wear practically every day."

"And Sundays?" asked Lindsay.

"Well, on Sundays I'd . . ." Melissa stopped. "What about Sundays?"

"If you were Laurie, your Sundays would be quite different. There'd be boating, fishing, camping, the zoo, but certainly no church. And forget about Sunday School and Junior Choir. I'm afraid you wouldn't get in on any of those things."

"Laurie's family doesn't go to church," Melissa nodded sadly. "There are no family devotions or any Bible talks in her home. Her family doesn't think it's necessary."

Lindsay nodded grimly. "Laurie has everything, except the most important thing. God hasn't left you high and dry, Melissa. He's given you parents who saw to it that you were baptized. He's given you a strong faith to trust in his forgiveness of sins."

"A pretty nose and hair don't seem all that important when you put it that way."

"It seems you could help Laurie along to find an inner beauty by showing her Christ," Lindsay suggested.

Instead of envying another person's blessings, let us thank God for the love he has shown us all in sending Jesus into the world to be our Savior. There is nothing we really lack as long as he is ours and we are his.

Prayer: Dear Jesus, forgive me for being jealous of other people. Thank you for dying on the cross to take away my sins. No matter what I look like or how smart I am or what I have, remind me I have true happiness when I have you as my Savior. Amen.

Passing The Buck

Then I heard the voice of the Lord saying, "Whom shall I send? And who will go for us?" And I said, "Here am I. Send me!" (Isaiah 6:8)

"I see you're practicing for Sunday," Michael said, grinning at Jason, who was quietly strumming his guitar.

Jason shot Michael an irritated glance. "What happens on Sunday?" their father asked, putting down his paper.

"Jason's been asked to play his guitar for the Sunday School opening."

Dad whistled in admiration. "This *is* quite an honor."

Jason flinched. "I told Pastor I couldn't do it," he said softly, glaring at Michael.

"Not doing it?" asked Dad. "Why not?"

"Stage fright," Jason answered lightly. "Too much stress is hard on the heart, Dad."

"Oh, Jason," Dad grinned. "Your heart is strong enough to withstand a slight case of nerves. Think how excited the children will be to sing with a new instrument."

"They like singing with the piano, and Judy Collins wants to play."

"But Pastor asked you," Dad reminded him.

"I think you should just change his name to Moses," Michael suggested. "No guts, just excuses."

"Moses didn't even play the guitar!" Jason replied in irritation.

"Maybe not, but he had a million reasons why he couldn't lead the Israelites out of Egypt," Michael answered. "He had a simple case of stage fright, just like you."

"I think you're being a little hard on your brother," Dad said, giving his younger son a firm glance. "But what would have happened if God had listened to Moses' excuses and let him back down?"

"Easy, God would have found another guy to fill in."

"Not so easy," Dad corrected Jason. "There was no one with the same background and training or the strong faith and humble spirit Moses had. God wanted him because he was right for the job!"

"Even if Moses didn't *feel* right for the job?" Jason asked.

"By giving Moses those special signs and his brother Aaron to help him speak, God showed Moses he would *make* him right for the job."

"I understand how important Moses' job was, but why is my guitar playing so important?" asked Jason.

"With your guitar you can praise the Lord, show your love for him, and really be a part of the worship. Saying yes now will also get you into the habit of saying yes later on. What would happen if Christians would always say no when God asked them to do something difficult?"

"I suppose God's work wouldn't get done. There'd be no pastors, no teachers, no children inviting friends to Sunday School. Everyone would think it's too scary to talk about Jesus," Jason reasoned. He paused. "I really do want to help, Dad, but how do I keep my hands from shaking?"

"First you must keep your heart from shaking," Dad answered. "A courageous heart is a gift from God. God will give it to you if you ask him in prayer. Remember, Jason, God never asks us to do anything without supplying his help. He forgave our sins, preparing us for heaven, and he continues to give us his help each day of our lives."

A tiny glimmer of courage sparked in Jason's eyes as he nodded and picked up his guitar once again.

Prayer: Dear Jesus, very often when I'm asked to serve you, I say no. It's not that I don't want to, but I'm scared. Turn my fear into courage so that I may carry out your will in my life. Amen.

Never Enough

Sorrowful, yet always rejoicing; poor, yet making many rich; having nothing, and yet possessing everything. (2 Corinthians 6:10)

Jason set his small package on the coffee table and slumped back onto the couch, still brooding over his small purchase. "Hey, Jason!" Michael called. "Did you get the new tires and inner tubes you wanted?"

"I could have bought half a new bike with what it cost me for tubes and tires!" he moaned.

"Except you'd look pretty ridiculous riding around town on half of a bike," grinned his younger brother.

Jason's mouth twitched, but he didn't smile. "I wish just once I could come out of a store satisfied with what I got for my money!"

"Not me," grinned Michael. "I wish I could come out of a store richer than when I walked in."

"Actually, there is a store like the one you've described," Mom said to Michael, as she stepped into the room. "At this store we can buy all we want and never go broke."

"It's a store on an alien planet, right, Mom?" Jason grinned.

"No, not at all," Mom answered, "In fact, they are found right here on our own planet earth, in our own town. We can have our fill of everything on this store's shelves and always get more. Best of all, we can come out richer than when we walked in."

"C'mon, Mom," Michael shook his head. "If this store is so marvelous, why haven't we heard about it before?"

"Oh, you've heard about it, Michael. You just haven't thought about it in exactly this way. I'm talking about church."

"Church?" asked Jason, as his voice dropped slightly. "Aw, Mom, we thought you were talking about a real store, a money store."

"Yeah, Mom," Michael groaned. "We thought you knew of a place to buy two new bike tires for nothing."

"No, church doesn't specialize in bike tires," Mom agreed. "I just wanted you boys to realize your hopes don't have to be shattered because you don't have the money to buy everything you want."

Jason nodded. "Dad says, it's a fact of life. Human beings never have enough money to buy all the things they want."

"Even if this is true, God doesn't want us to become sad and depressed about not having what our hearts desire. He wants us to realize there is another store more important than a money store. Our true heart's desire should be found in church, where we hear the preaching of God's word, where the gospel is publicly proclaimed."

"I still don't understand though how church can be a store," Michael persisted.

"Well, you can walk into church very empty, feeling so sad about your sins and feeling troubled over the difficulties of life, but when you come out you are a happier person," Mom explained.

Michael nodded. "We are happier because we hear that our sin is forgiven through Jesus. There are no price tags keeping forgiveness of sins from anyone, rich or poor."

146

Mom nodded. "Remember, though, forgiveness of sins is only free to us because Jesus gave up his life on the cross for it. He paid the highest price for our forgiveness, so we could have it free of charge!"

Jason opened his tiny bag and emptied its contents. "It's ridiculous to get so upset over expensive bike tires. It's not like it'll ruin my life," he grinned.

Mom nodded. "Some folks spend their whole life striving to get ahead, striving for money to make them happy. I want you boys to realize, rich or poor, you really have all you need in Jesus."

Prayer: Dear Jesus, I see grown-ups getting so upset about bills and money. Help me, as I get older, to realize money can never bring me true happiness. Help me to see true contentment is found in the forgiveness of my sins. Amen.

Shipshape

But godliness with contentment is great gain. For we brought nothing into the world, and we can take nothing out of it. But if we have food and clothing, we will be content with that. (1 Timothy 6:6-8)

Michael curiously watched his sister unwrap the chewy stick of gum and pop it into her mouth. Before he could speak, Dad bolted upright in his chair. "This is amazing" he declared, grasping the newspaper tightly. "The owner of Shipshape Supermarket was just indicted on fifteen counts of embezzlement."

"Shipshape?" Mom asked. "I shop for groceries there every week."

"According to this article, everything hasn't been exactly shipshape at the store. Over a five-year period, Mr. Goodbody evidently stole $20,000 from his customers by telling his cashiers to add items to their receipts, even though the items hadn't been purchased."

"Well, of all the nerve!" Melissa exclaimed. "Mr. Goodbody might as well have broken into our house and taken our money. It would have been the same thing!" She snapped her gum emphatically.

Curiously, Michael watched his twin sister's busy jaw. "What a rotten guy Mr. Goodbody is!" Jason exclaimed, popping a very large round pink bubble. "He certainly is nothing like his name!"

"I just wonder how much of that $20,000 belongs to us!" Lindsay complained.

Listening to his brother and sisters' protests, Michael frowned. "So you think Mr. Goodbody is a real crook?" asked Michael. "What about you guys? You take a pack of gum off of a guy's dresser without asking. It may not be $20,000, but to me it's stealing just the same!"

Michael's words stabbed at his brother and sisters' consciences. Whether it's a walletful of money or a tiny piece of gum, stealing is wrong. Such sins start as a little rebellion in the heart, a tiny bit of greed which says, "I want it. I will take it. No matter what, I have to be satisfied." And this thoughtless, greedy heart is not concerned about the sorrow that its stealing causes someone else.

How are we able to deal with a greedy heart which constantly wants? Will flipping through the toy catalog make us less greedy? Will constant trips to the mall quench our desire to have? Doing these things may only feed our greedy appetites, making us feel emptier when we can't have everything we want.

A greedy heart can only be changed to a caring heart if God does the changing. God shows us in his word that money

148

can't take sins away; money can't give us lasting happiness; money can't buy what we truly need and crave. God asks every one of us, "What good will it be for a man if he gains the whole world, yet forfeits his soul? Or what can a man give in exchange for his soul" (Matthew 16:26)? We could possess all the money in the world, but if our sins aren't forgiven and our souls connected to Christ, we would be doomed to everlasting punishment.

Do you see how important it is to fight our greedy hearts? Instead of dreaming of skateboards, candy, clothes, and toys, let us concentrate on the love Jesus showed us by dying on the cross for our sins. Window-shopping, catalog-thumbing, and mall-hopping leave us spiritually empty. Satisfying our hunger with Jesus' life, death, and resurrection leaves us filled. It turns a greedy, thoughtless, heart into a heart which wants to show that same, selfless love to others.

Prayer: Dear Jesus, I am sorry I have let my heart become greedy at times. I know things can only leave me feeling empty. Your forgiveness is what I truly need. Help me to desire you most of all. Amen.

Yes

For no matter how many promises God has made, they are "Yes" in Christ. (2 Corinthians 1:20)

Melissa walked back and forth in front of the front door. Her roller skates were slung over her shoulder. Every few seconds she peered out the front door.

"Dad," Michael complained. "Melissa's wearing out the rug again," he teased. "Would you tell her to stop her ridiculous pacing?"

Melissa glared at her brother and took a seat in the chair near the front door. "I wouldn't be pacing if I'd know for sure that Carol's mother is going to pick me up. Carol said she'd come *if* the washer repair man was gone by five, *if* the baby was down for a late nap, and *if* the older children had finished their homework. I really wish my happiness didn't depend on Carol's mother. There are just too many if's with her. I wish I could just hear a solid 'yes' once in a while."

Does your happiness often seem to depend upon other people? As children who don't receive a regular paycheck every week and who don't have the freedom to come and go as we please, it often seems our happiness does depend on others. Like Melissa, we'd rather hear a solid "yes" than a lot of "maybes" from those we depend upon.

This is exactly how the Corinthian Christians felt long ago. These believers had waited eagerly for their dear pastor, the apostle Paul, to come for a visit. His preaching about the Lord Jesus Christ had brought many of them to faith. He had made plans to visit them. But travel was much more difficult in those days than it is today. Paul couldn't just hop a plane and come to his friends. Just as Melissa waited and wondered if Carol's mother would come, these believers also waited and wondered if Paul would come. It seemed as if their total happiness depended upon Paul's coming.

The apostle Paul wrote a letter to them to set matters straight. He wanted them to realize that, even if he couldn't give them a definite, "Yes, I will come," they were not to become worried. Even if weather, shipwreck, or death kept Paul away from them, they still could know that God's promises would remain true.

Are you worried about finding a Christian friend or doing well in school? Are you worried about your future? Do you wonder who it is you will marry, or whether or not you will be able to find a Christian husband or wife? Are you especially concerned about the many sins you have committed?

We can't depend upon other people for our total happiness, but we can depend upon God. He has promised to forgive our wrongdoing. He has promised to be with us while we are growing up. He promises he will never leave us nor forsake us, no matter what troubles or dangers come into our lives.

In Jesus Christ we are safe. He died on the cross. He rose from the dead. He gives us forgiveness of sins and life forever in heaven. With people, it is sometimes "yes," sometimes "no," and many times "maybe." But with God it is always a definite and solid "Yes."

Prayer: Dear Jesus, I thank you that all my real happiness depends upon you. I know I can trust you to forgive my sins, to always be with me here on earth, and to give me life in heaven. Remind me never to depend upon anyone else but you. Amen.

Shout It From The Mountain Tops

I tell you, whoever acknowledges me before men, the Son of Man will also acknowledge him before the angels of God. **(Luke 12:8)**

The Anderson family sat at the large corner booth of their favorite restaurant. The hot food had just arrived, but before tasting it, the family bowed their heads. With folded hands, they prayed their familiar table prayer in quiet voices. Instead of whispering the prayer with the others, however, five-year-old Tracy prayed in her normal speaking voice. In fact, at the end of the prayer, her "Amen" rang loudly throughout the restaurant.

She smacked her lips, picked up her fork, and stabbed her meat hungrily. Jason and Lindsay looked from side to side, noticing that many eyes were staring at them. "Don't you know we're not at home?" scolded Lindsay. "Everyone is looking at us. Couldn't you pray just a little more quietly?" she whispered.

Tracy blinked uncertainly. "But I always pray out loud at home. Why do I have to whisper here? Is this place like the restaurant in Whispering Town?"

Lindsay frowned impatiently. "What is Whispering Town?"

Michael brightened. "It's not a real town. It's a town in a book. In Whispering Town no one speaks above a whisper. Even the trains, whistles, and fire sirens whisper."

"Once a little boy visited Whispering Town and decided it was just plain silly to whisper when he had a perfectly good talking voice," Tracy added. "Is this restaurant like Whispering Town?" Tracy asked her daddy with wide, pleading eyes.

Dad's eyes were twinkling. "Tracy, I have to tell you, there is no real place like Whispering Town. But, sometimes when Christians are around people who may not believe in Jesus as their Savior, ordinary places can turn into Whispering Towns."

"Why do they?" asked Tracy.

"Sometimes Christians are afraid of what others might think when they show they love and honor Jesus. They're afraid they'll be made fun of, afraid they'll get peculiar stares."

"But, if we talk in whispers all the time, how will anyone hear that Jesus died for their sins, too?"

Whispering Town—have you ever acted as if you were in its city limits when you had a chance to boldly proclaim Jesus as your Savior? When the prophet Elijah was about to be taken into heaven by the whirlwind of fiery horses and chariot, Elisha asked God to give him a double portion of Elijah's spirit. Elisha realized he couldn't be a successful preacher of the gospel if he was afraid to show others their sin and also point them to Jesus as the forgiver of all sins.

152

On our own, we all are whispering Christians, afraid to speak what we know and believe is the truth. But with God's help we can become as bold as Elijah and Elisha, unafraid to let others know we trust in Jesus as our Savior. Instead of being cowardly whispering Christians, may God in Christ make us bold, shouting the good news of our Savior even from the mountain tops.

Prayer:
Ashamed of Jesus? Yes, I may
When I've no guilt to wash away,
No tear to wipe, no good to crave,
No fear to quell, no soul to save.

Till then—nor is my boasting vain—
Till then I boast a Savior slain;
And oh, may this my glory be,
That Christ is not ashamed of me! (TLH 346:5,6)

That Old Wagging Tongue

Brothers, do not slander one another. (James 4:11)

"Did anyone see Sharon in P.E. today?" giggled one of Lindsay's friends. "She wore her P.E. uniform inside out!"

"Sharon is so peculiar. She probably didn't even notice."

"She doesn't notice much, especially what's in style. Look at the way she wears her hair. Do you think she had it buzzed?"

"I have no idea, but where does she buy her clothes? They all are outdated and twice her size."

"She thinks everybody likes her, especially the boys. She pretends to forget her locker key every day, so Joey Phillips can open it for her. I think she's in love with him."

"Joey's her cousin," Lindsay replied quietly. "Her clothes are old and big because her parents lost everything they owned in a fire this summer. Her hair wasn't buzzed; it was burned in the fire. Her parents couldn't scrape enough money together for new glasses, and Sharon is terribly nearsighted. That's why she keeps losing her key all the time. As for her P.E. uniform, the factory sewed the buttons on the inside. She could only button it by wearing it inside out."

"Have you heard Sharon play the piano? Have you heard her sing? Have you noticed she can run the fastest mile in the whole school? Sharon's sister was blinded by the fire, and Sharon tutors her every night after school. Sharon's my friend, and your gossip is worse than the fire that took away her house, her hair, and her belongings. You're burning a hole in the only thing she has left—her good name!"

"Did you really say *all that* at Denise's pajama party?" asked Melissa Anderson when Lindsay retold the story to the family.

Lindsay nodded. "It's the reason I left the party, too. I couldn't stand to listen to my friends tear down Sharon's reputation. Why do they find so much joy in destroying someone's good name?"

"Your friends must think that by tearing Sharon down they can boost themselves up. With their gossip they are trying to bury their own faults under Sharon's," Mom explained.

"They have to dig pretty deep to say anything bad about Sharon. She has so many wonderful qualities," Lindsay answered.

"Perhaps Sharon's talents make your friends feel inadequate. Gossip is a very clever tool of Satan. Gossip can even be the truth or use the truth, but often it is twisted truth, or the truth only in part. Gossip always condemns. It never congratulates. It brings out all the bad and buries the good."

"How do I stop gossip?" asked Lindsay.

"It can be stopped by speaking up for a person, just as you spoke up for Sharon tonight." Dad explained.

154

"But, there's another problem, Dad. Just as the girls made fun of Sharon, I'm afraid Jesus' name is still being mocked and ridiculed. I hear it happen at school, on TV, even when I'm walking through the mall," Lindsay complained.

"Then, just as you stuck up for Sharon, your friend, you especially ought to stick up for Jesus, your Savior. No one would know what a beautiful person Sharon is without your words, and no one will realize Jesus is really our glorious, powerful, and loving Savior unless we speak up."

Prayer: Dear Jesus, please forgive me when I gossip. Forgive me for trying to make myself look better by ruining another person's good name. Thank you for forgiving my faults instead of broadcasting my sins to everyone. Amen.

Putting Out The Welcome Mat

Slaves, submit yourselves to your masters with all respect, not only to those who are good and considerate, but also to those who are harsh. (1 Peter 2:18)

Melissa set her book bag on the counter. The corners of her mouth drooped pathetically. "Hard day at the office?" winked her brother.

"Neither of us is in the mood for humor," Michael responded coldly. "We had a substitute teacher today."

"I don't think she was a real teacher," sniffed Melissa. "Real teachers like kids. The only time I saw her smile was when she was assigning homework. She thinks we are her slaves."

"I worked for a boss once who was exactly the same way," Mom answered, setting a bowl of fruit on the counter. "My boss was never pleasant, always suspicious, and she barked out commands. It was hard not to join in with the other

155

employees, talking about her behind her back, taking longer coffee breaks to get even, or simply being disrespectful toward her."

"What did you do?" asked Melissa.

"I knew if I showed the same disrespect, I wouldn't make God very happy. I also realized that treating her badly would only make her grumpier."

"But she treated you so badly. She didn't deserve any respect."

"Maybe not in the eyes of the world, but in the eyes of God she did, because it was God who put her over me. I remembered, too, that, when Jesus died on the cross to save me, I didn't do anything to deserve such kindness. If God could be so kind to me by sending his Son, Jesus, to be my Savior, it was only right for me to be kind to someone he had placed over me, even if she was a harsh boss."

"Have you tried treating your sub just like your regular teacher?" asked Lindsay. "You are constantly drawing or writing sweet little notes to Miss Kasten. Why not try it on your sub?"

"Why not try putting out the welcome mat for her, so that she feels like she is appreciated?" asked Mom.

Michael nodded. "Today I'm sure all she saw from us was the unwelcome mat," he admitted.

What kind of mat do you put out for those God has placed over you? Do you purposely make your parents' and teachers' lives difficult? Our disrespectful or unkind actions pierce our Savior's heart, because our parents and Christian teachers are the ones he has given to us to teach us how we are saved. We may not like how they dress or act or discipline us all the time, but it is through them that we are brought to the Lord. How can they successfully bring us the word of God, if we are constantly fighting them?

By our courteous, respectful words and kind actions we show our love to God who placed our parents and teachers over us. By showing such a humble attitude we may not be able to soften a harsh personality, but our Christ-like behavior is seen by our Heavenly Father. He understands and is pleased by this way of thanking him for sending his Son to be our Savior.

Prayer: Dear Jesus, sometimes when my elders seem harsh to me, I use that as an excuse to be disrespectful toward them. Forgive me, and make me as humble and kind as you have always been to me. Amen.

Afraid To Share?

Offer hospitality to one another without grumbling. Each one should use whatever gift he has received to serve others, faithfully administering God's grace in its various forms. (1 Peter 4:9,10)

Melissa Anderson took a bite out of her cookie, turned it over in her mouth, and relished the chocolate goodness. "Oh-oh!" her friend Carol cried, bumping her arm. "Look who's coming."

Melissa squinted into the sun as she tried to observe the sidewalk which ran parallel to her house. "It's Christa Bloom.

She and her brothers pass by every Saturday on their way to swimming lessons. What's wrong with that?"

Carol gobbled her cookie down and grabbed another. "Every Saturday they come by, and every Saturday we have to share our snack," she grumbled. "I'm ducking into the playhouse so I won't have to share!"

Carol quickly slipped off the back step and hurried toward the playhouse. Melissa stared at the plate of cookies and the approaching children now only a half block away. "I'll have plenty of time to slip into the playhouse without anyone finding out," Melissa thought.

As she turned to go, Melissa spotted her mother through the screen door. Mrs. Anderson was preparing a basket of fruit for the new neighbors who had just moved in down the street. Melissa smiled. With all her brothers and sisters to feed, Mom never hesitated to share what she had.

"If we obey God and look out for others, God will surely look out for us," Mom would often say. "Isn't it God who knows our needs? Isn't it God who gives us everything we have?"

Melissa looked down at the plate. The cookies she and Carol were trying to hoard weren't even their own. Mom had made them. Carol's favorite words of advice were, "You have to watch out for number one." Were she and Carol really number one? Were their wants and desires more important than anyone else's?

The only person who could honestly label himself number one was Jesus Christ, the almighty Son of God. He has power over heaven and earth. Yet, even he in his lifetime never lorded it over anyone. He never hesitated to put others first. He became a servant to us all and gave up his life on the cross for our sins.

Melissa listened as her mother quietly hummed a hymn. Wasn't it because of Jesus' selfless suffering and death for her sins that Mom shared so much? She wanted others to feel just as important and loved as God made her feel when he forgave her sins.

Christa Bloom and her brothers were only a few yards away now. With determination, Melissa jumped off the back step, grabbed the tiny plate of cookies, and walked over to them.

Are you afraid to share the blessings God has given to you? In our selfishness we often think that we won't have all the happiness and enjoyment we want if we share. That day Melissa found out she acquired more happiness by doing what pleased God.

If Melissa had ducked into the playhouse, she would have finished the cookies with a guilty conscience. If she hadn't shared her snack, Christa Bloom may not have thought to invite her to her birthday party on Saturday. If she hadn't shared her cookies and been so happy about the party, she may not have felt bold enough to ask Christa to Sunday School. Three tiny cookies on a plate. Shared, they grew into much happiness for many.

Prayer: Dear Jesus, I am so selfish sometimes with my belongings. Remind me they are all gifts from you. Take away my selfishness and help me to share. Help me also to share my faith with others that they, too, may know you as their Savior. Amen.

What Is Real?

This is my body which is given to you. . . . This cup is the new covenant in my blood which is poured out for you. (Luke 22:19,20)

Michael sank his teeth into a large piece of pizza. "Hmmm!" he exclaimed. "I could eat pizza every day of the week."

Melissa also took a bite of pizza. Unlike her brother, she

pushed her plate away and made a face. "I don't know how they can even call this pizza, with this imitation cheese smothering it!"

Lindsay examined her slice. "How can you tell? It looks like the real thing." Lindsay smacked her lips after taking another bite. "It tastes like real mozzarella to me."

"But it doesn't have strings like real mozzarella!" Melissa argued.

"And it doesn't have the 'Real Seal' on the package!" Jason added.

Just like the cheese on the Anderson's pizza, there are countless foods in the grocery store which are imitation. It looks and tastes like butter, but it's not. It looks and tastes like juice, but it's not. It looks and tastes like fish, but it's not. With so many imitation products for sale, it is very hard to tell what is real and what is fake. This is the reason many foods carry the "Real Seal."

There are also two sacraments which we celebrate in church which carry the "Real Seal." These sacraments are baptism and the Lord's Supper. Many of you have seen a little child or an adult baptized in your church. When the pastor sprinkles a person with water and speaks God's word, how do you know a true baptism is taking place? How do you know the person is truly receiving forgiveness from his or her sins?

Many of you have also seen your parents and grandparents take part in the Lord's Supper. With your eyes you only see the bread and wine they receive. How do you know they have truly received Christ's body and blood for the forgiveness of sins?

With our eyes it isn't always possible to tell what is real and what is fake. Just as we must check the "Real Seal" on pizza and other foods, we must also check the "Real Seal" of the sacraments. This "Real Seal" is found in God's word. In Acts 2:38 God speaks of the power of baptism with these words: "Repent and be baptized, every one of you, in the name of Jesus Christ *for the forgiveness of your sins.*"

160

We also understand the Lord's Supper is not imitation when God tells us in Luke 22:19,20: "This *is* my body given for you. . . . This cup *is* the new covenant in my blood which is poured out for you." When Jesus spoke these words, he was telling us his body and blood are truly present in the bread and wine. In Ephesians 1:7 God also spoke through the apostle Paul: "In him (Jesus) we have redemption through his blood, the forgiveness of sins." Since we are receiving Christ's body and blood in the bread and wine, we are also receiving the forgiveness from our sins. There is no imitation. In baptism and the Lord's Supper we receive Jesus' forgiveness, just as we do when we hear the word of God. Even though you cannot see God's power, you know it is there. It is God's promise as found in the Bible, and this, too, is real.

Prayer: Dear Jesus, give me a strong faith so I never doubt the power you placed in baptism and the Lord's Supper to forgive my sins. Remind me that you are the one who has given it the power for my salvation. Amen.

When Forgiving Comes Hard

All that the Father gives me will come to me, and whoever comes to me I will never drive away. (John 6:37)

"Lindsay!" Jason called. "Sandy Russell is on the phone."

"Tell her I'll call back when I'm not so busy," Lindsay replied.

Mom looked up from her mending. "You don't look extremely busy to me right now," she chuckled. "Are you too comfortable with your book to talk to a friend?"

"Sandy may be a lot of things, but friend is not one of them," Lindsay replied evenly. "Do you remember the poetry contest I entered?"

"Sure," Mom replied. "Have they announced the winners yet?"

"Yes," Lindsay answered. She searched through the newspaper rack and folded the school paper open to the poetry section.

Mom beamed happily. "Look, Lindsay, your poem won second place. Why didn't you tell us?"

"Look who the author is," Lindsay complained.

"Sandy Russell? Why is her name at the bottom of your poem?"

"She copied mine, almost word for word. When I sent my own poem in, the staff wouldn't believe it was my work."

"Now I understand why you didn't want to talk to Sandy," Mom answered, "but what if she is calling to apologize?"

Lindsay sighed angrily. "I'm not sure I am ready to forgive."

"Do you want to make her suffer a little longer?" Mom asked.

"It's only fair, Mom. Sandy's nearly ruined my reputation."

"Forgiving never comes easily, but if we want to call ourselves children of God, forgiving has to be a very important part of our Christian lives." Mom paused. "Just lately I've been reading quite a bit from the Old Testament. I came across a certain really bad character by the name of Manasseh. He was a king of Judah after his father Hezekiah."

"I've never heard of a Manasseh who was a king," Lindsay replied.

Mom explained. "This Manasseh was a murdering, bloodthirsty king. He worshiped Baal and the stars. He practiced witchcraft and even sacrificed his own sons to a false god in the fire. He shed so much innocent blood that the Bible tells us he filled Jerusalem from end to end with it."

"What did God do to him?" Lindsay asked in horror.

"God dealt with Manasseh the same way he deals with us. In spite of all of his sins, God still loved him. God hoped that by punishing him severely he could wake up Manasseh and turn him away from his wickedness. God sent the Assyrian army to Jerusalem, and they took Manasseh prisoner. They put a hook in his nose and bound him with bronze shackles and sent him off to Babylon. There Manasseh did finally humble himself, and he prayed to God for forgiveness."

"Did God listen even after he had committed so many terrible sins?" Lindsay asked.

Mom nodded. "God could read Manasseh's heart, and he saw how truly sorry he was. God restored him to his kingship. Manasseh showed his thankfulness and obedience to God by getting rid of the foreign gods."

"Manasseh didn't deserve all of God's mercy after what he had done," Lindsay answered.

"No," Mom agreed, "but neither do we. If we are honest, we must admit that we, too, have done some pretty horrible sins. Our thoughts are impure. We've even committed murder in God's eyes many times by our hatred and unloving ways. Jesus has forgiven us so much. I wonder how he feels when we find it too hard to forgive."

Lindsay swallowed slowly. "He might think we don't appreciate how much suffering he went through on the cross to forgive our many sins." Lindsay paused and then replied quietly. "I think I'll give Sandy a call now. When I need forgiving, I don't want God to be too busy for me."

Prayer: Dear Jesus, sometimes forgiving is a very tough job for me. When someone sins against me, I want to hold on to my anger. Help me, instead, to forgive as you have forgiven me. Let this be my way of showing thankfulness to you. Amen.

Short Fuse

The LORD is compassionate and gracious, slow to anger, abounding in love. (Psalm 103:8)

Jason lay sprawled across the family room couch, enjoying the newspaper's comics. Little Tracy knelt before the coffee table, toying with the new airplane Michael had received for his birthday. Michael suddenly burst through the door, looking for his new plane. His heart raced when he saw his little sister's clumsy fingers touching his prize birthday present.

"What are you doing touching my plane?" he screamed. With four swift strides he raced across the room to rescue his precious property. Tracy's face turned red; her lips trembled. Suddenly she burst into tears. Covering her face to hold back the sobs, she ran from the room.

Jason glared at his younger brother. He clicked his tongue disapprovingly. Michael returned the glare. "Well, what was I supposed to do?"

"You could have been a little gentler. She's only five."

Michael shook his head. "The long and short of it is that Tracy shouldn't be fooling with my things!"

"The real long and short of it is that you are long on anger and short on patience. You have an extremely short fuse, Michael."

"Can you blame me?" he snapped back. "She broke the wing flap clean off."

"A little more patience would have kept you from yanking it out of her hand."

"When she touches my things, I stop owing her any patience at all!"

"Dad could have treated you the same way last week when you broke his new saw blade. He didn't even yell. Neither did Lindsay when you broke the kickstand on her bike. And what about this morning when you spilled your milk and broke the glass?"

"Mom had to change her skirt because most of my milk

164

spilled on her lap," Michael admitted, as if he were recalling the facts for the first time. "How could they all be so patient with me? I deserved a few sharp words at least."

"And more!" Jason exclaimed, "but Dad, Mom, and Lindsay love you and wanted to forgive you."

"But none of them even mentioned again what I had done," Michael answered. "Do they all have short memories?"

"I don't think so," Jason said. "Every time they think about bringing it up, they remember the times they have hurt someone. They especially recall how patient Jesus is to forgive all of their sins. Slow to anger, that's how the Bible describes the way God treats us."

"We really deserve God's anger to explode every time we sin."

"But his love makes him patient and kind. He gives us every chance to seek forgiveness. Instead of showing his anger, he wants to forgive us."

"I wish I wouldn't have yelled at Tracy," Michael announced. "What can I do now? The words are out. Should I give her my plane to play with?"

"Of course not," Jason answered. "Your new plane is too fragile for a kindergartner to play with. It can be broken too easily. Instead, you could quietly explain it to her, dry her tears, and find some way to show her you still care about her."

Michael nodded. "I get it. Being patient doesn't mean I have to give her everything she wants. It means I should treat her in a caring way."

"Sure, and while you are being slow with your anger, I'll have time to fix this broken wing flap," winked Jason.

"You don't have to do that," Michael smiled.

"I know, but it doesn't hurt me to be long on patience once in a while, either," he replied.

Prayer: Dear Jesus, I often have a problem controlling my temper. When someone hurts me, my anger explodes. Please forgive me for not being patient as you are with me. Help me to be slow to anger and quick to forgive. Amen.

A Little Exercise

For physical training is of some value, but godliness has value for all things, holding promise for both the present life and the life to come. **(1 Timothy 4:8)**

"Lindsay! Lindsay!" called Melissa as she entered the room the girls shared. "Mom says you beat Susan Alcott in the 100-meter dash this morning."

"Such a long time ago," moaned a dull, listless voice from under a pile of pillows and blankets. "I feel awful now. Dr. Franke says I've caught some sort of virus."

"Well, don't worry. In a couple of days you'll be stepping into your running shoes again," Melissa assured her sister as she strapped her feet into the ski machine blocks.

Lindsay listened to the mesmerizing click-click of the heavy machine as she watched her sister's graceful movements. "Exercise bike, trampoline, Dad's weight machine, and now the ski machine; maybe I take exercise a little too seriously. If a little germ can make a strong body this useless, maybe I've been wasting my time."

"Couch potatoes get sick, too, Lindsay. You know a healthy body can fight sickness better than a weak body."

"Sure, but is a certain amount of exercise ever too much?"

Melissa unstrapped her feet from the ski apparatus. "It can only be too much if a person begins to think he is *only* a body—if he forgets the soul part of him. Mom says our sicknesses help us remember the soul part of us."

Have you ever forgotten that there are two parts which make you a person? We are very concerned with developing our bodies, but our souls are equally important. Aerobics and weight machines have no power to develop the spiritual side of us. Having a strong and faithful spirit in an energetic body comes about only by hearing God's word.

Lindsay discovered a simple fever could zap her body of much of its strength. In the same way, the problems we face in life are able to zap our faith. Just as a strong body fights off germs faster, so a faith which has been built up by the power of God's word will not crumble when troubles come.

Jesus died for you on the cross. He died to save you, body and soul. When you die, your body will die, but your soul goes to be with Jesus. Later, on Judgment Day your body will reunite with your soul.

Keeping your body in good shape is another way of thanking God for giving you your body. After all, it's the only body you will ever have. Just as you are careful to feed and exercise your body, be careful also to exercise and feed your soul through the word of God. We exercise our souls when we concentrate daily on that holy and selfless love, which God showered upon us by dying on the cross to forgive our sins.

Remember to concentrate on the most valuable part of you. Your body dies, but your soul lives on forever.

There can be no dispute. A strong body is valuable, but a strong spirit which relies on Jesus' grace and forgiveness is priceless.

Prayer: Dear Jesus, forgive me when I seem so interested in keeping my body strong and so careless when it comes to the shape my faith is in. Give me a stronger love for your Word. I need you as my Savior. Amen.

Our Judge, Loving, But Fair

God was reconciling the world to himself in Christ, not counting men's sins against them. And he has committed to us the message of reconciliation. (2 Corinthians 5:19)

Michael sat very still on a high step-stool in the center of the playroom. He was dressed in a long, flowing robe and held a small hammer in his hand. Beside him on a much smaller stool sat little Tracy who held her chubby little hands over her eyes and pretended to cry.

Suddenly the laundry room door swung open. Out stepped Melissa, dressed in one of Mom's old skirts. As she cleared her throat, the room quieted. "It is true, your Honor, that my client, Tracy Anderson, threw dirty socks under the bed as charged," Melissa began. "Yet, with this little scale, I, her lawyer, will attempt to show she has more than made up for her crime!"

"I have labeled her crime 'Exhibit A,'" Melissa announced. She placed a small weight labeled "A, dirty socks under bed" on the scale. "Exhibits B, C, and D!" she called triumphantly, setting three more weights on the other side of the scale. On these weights she had written, "Pulled Mrs. Hobb's cat out of the tree," "Turned off the stove before meat boiled over," and "Found Dad's lost keys."

"Notice how the scale tips under the weight of all these good deeds?" Melissa said to the judge. "Having seen this demonstration, I am sure that our faithful judge will declare Miss Tracy innocent of this small, insignificant crime of having dirty, disgusting socks under the bed!"

The judge looked down sternly at Tracy and then at her lawyer. "Clever, quite clever reasoning. Yet, dirty socks are dirty socks. No matter how insignificant, they are still under the bed and they still are dirty! Tracy is guilty as charged," Michael cried, banging the small hammer on his desk. "Pay the bailiff on the way out. Next case!"

"I object!" Melissa cried. "Are you saying all the good my client has done is worthless? What kind of judge are you?"

"A fair one, I can assure you, my dear, frightfully fair!"

"Mom!" Melissa complained. "Michael isn't very understanding. He won't consider all the good things Tracy has done. He stubbornly insists on being fair."

Mom smiled as she stepped out of the laundry roam. "I'm afraid Michael is right, Melissa. All the good things Tracy has done do not erase the dirty socks thrown under the bed. Guilty as charged!" Mom called, hitting the table with Michael's tiny hammer.

Melissa thought her brother was a cold and cruel judge. Many people feel the same way about God. They think God has no right to hold them responsible for their sins if they have tried to do the best they could to make up for their sins. Melissa was totally surprised when Michael handed down the guilty verdict. How much more surprised will people be when God pronounces the guilty verdict on their sins.

No amount of good we have done can make up for the bad we do. All sin must be punished, or God wouldn't be a fair and holy judge. Yet, God is neither cold nor cruel. He thought of a way to satisfy his holiness as well as his love for us. He sent his pure and holy Son, Jesus, to pay for the sins we had done. Jesus was punished in our place on the cross.

In play-acting, it was Tracy's own judge and brother, Michael, who lovingly pulled the dirty socks out from under the bed and threw them into the hamper. In real life, it was our judge Jesus Christ who led the perfect life we couldn't and who paid the punishment for our sins on the cross. May we always uphold his fairness and praise him for his great love.

Prayer: Dear Jesus, forgive me when I think the good things I do can make up for the bad things I have done. I know it isn't true. I need your forgiveness, pure and simple. Thank you for saving me. I couldn't have done it on my own. Amen.

What Is Really Valuable?

The world and its desires pass away, but the man who does the will of God lives forever. (1 John 2:17)

"Hey, Michael! Where did you get that expensive camera?" asked Melissa. "Did you borrow it?"

"No, not at all. I pulled it out of Mr. Hobbs' trash. Can you believe he was going to throw it away? The lens isn't even scratched. Everything looks like it works. All I have to do is buy some film and . . ."

"But why would Mr. Hobbs just throw it away? He must have paid quite a bit of money for it," Melissa insisted.

Jason, who had been examining the camera over the twins' shoulders, shook his head sadly. "I'm afraid you'll have to throw it away for the same reason Mr. Hobbs did. They don't make film for this kind of camera any more."

Michael stared sadly at the expensive piece of equipment. "Still so new, still so shiny," he answered softly.

"New, shiny, and worthless," Jason agreed reluctantly.

Michael had been so excited to find such a treasure at the bottom of the neighbor's garbage can. Yet, without film the camera was useless and only fit for the trash barrel.

Everything that exists on this earth at the end of time will be just as worthless. The computer game we scrimped and saved for, the bicycle we couldn't live without, the outfit we couldn't get our mind off—these will be like so much garbage at the bottom of a trash barrel. These wonderful gadgets and beautiful treasures will no longer be of any use to any of us.

When Jesus comes again, he won't be interested in counting all the pretty outfits we have collected, or investigating the latest modern conveniences we've bought, or visiting the choicest restaurant on the planet.

Rather, Jesus will come to investigate hearts, to see what kind of shape they are in. Those who found joy only in gathering all the gadgets they could find and had no use for God and his gift of salvation will be sent to hell—the terrible place of torment prepared for the wicked angels.

However, Jesus will have heaven's door swing wide open to receive those in whose hearts he finds sorrow over sin and a real trust in his forgiveness.

Just as Michael examined the beautiful camera, let us also examine our hearts. God doesn't want us to throw away all of our earthly goods. We do need them while we live in this world. Yet, he wants us to know that they are useless in providing forgiveness of sins, and in bringing us eternal life in heaven.

With God's help, may we all keep our minds and hearts on things above instead of on things below.

Prayer: Dear Jesus, forgive me when I become too attached to the treasures of this world. Help me to remember they can never save my soul from hell, that only you can perform this miracle. Amen.

Why, God, Why?

The LORD gave and the LORD has taken away; may the name of the LORD be praised. (Job 1:21)

Tracy's tears poured down on her little puppy, Oliver. The driver of the speeding car hadn't even stopped to say he was sorry. Tracy cuddled her lifeless pet in her arms and carried him into the house.

"Why? Mommy, why?" Tracy cried, after her family had wrapped Oliver in a blanket and buried him in the back yard. "Why did God have to take my puppy away? Why didn't he protect him from that speeding car?"

"We don't always know why God lets a bad thing happen, Tracy. But we do know he makes all things turn out for our good."

Lindsay laid the potato peeler on the kitchen sink. "Remember last year when the Dawson's little four-year-old boy fell into their backyard pool and drowned? So many at his funeral were asking why God would let such a terrible thing happen."

"Until we get to heaven, we will never know for sure why God wanted to take little Tommy away just then," Mom answered. "But we can see already how Tommy's death has brought his parents closer to Jesus."

Lindsay nodded. "Hearing God's word is so very important to them now. They haven't missed a church service since Tommy's death."

How do you act when bad things happen? The Bible tells us of a man called Job, who in a single day lost everything he owned. God even took his children away from him. Instead of cursing God for what had happened, Job declared, "The LORD gave and the LORD has taken away; may the name of the LORD be praised."

Just like Job, our trust in Jesus should be strong. Our almighty God, who cared enough about us to die for our sins, knows what is best for us. He can look into the future and will work out everything the right way in order to see us safely into heaven.

Why did a speeding car run over little Oliver? Lindsay still thinks to this day that it could have been for Tracy's protection. Only God knows for sure, but the following day when Lindsay took her little sister to the park, a peculiar thing happened. Lindsay had climbed a tree to help untangle a little boy's kite string from the branches. While her back was turned, a stranger, who had been seated on a park bench, walked over to Tracy.

"Hi, little girl," he said, as he caught her at the bottom of the slide. "Didn't I see your cream-colored puppy run over that hill?"

Tracy looked up at him uncertainly. "Do I know you?" she asked.

"Well, sure you do, I come here all the time. I feel so bad

about your little dog running away. If you come with me, we'll find him over by my car. We wouldn't want him to get lost!"

"You're lying!" cried Tracy, stepping backwards. "You couldn't have seen Oliver run over that hill; he was hit by a car yesterday." Without another word, Tracy raced over to Lindsay.

Would Tracy have been fooled by this stranger if little Oliver hadn't died the day before? Only God knows why things happen as they do. As his believers, we can be sure that, whatever does happen in this life is for our everlasting good!

Prayer: Dear Jesus, please forgive me for getting angry at you when bad things happen to me. Help me to trust in you as my Savior with my whole heart. Amen.

Are You Stingy With God's Gifts?

Everything comes from you, and we have given you only what comes from your hand. (1 Chronicles 29:14)

"Melissa? Do you have the masking tape?" Mom asked as she stood in the doorway of her daughter's bedroom.

Mom needed no reply. As she peered into the room, her eyes met masking tape everywhere she looked. Two heavy lines of tape ran around Melissa's bed and continued around her bookcase. The column of tape proceeded around Melissa's study desk. As she looked more closely, Mrs. Anderson realized the tape also had been made into labels. These name tags appeared on every book, toy, hairbrush, comb and mirror that Melissa owned.

"Would you like to explain what you are doing?" Mom asked, noticing the roll of tape was practically gone.

"I'm marking my things," Melissa replied innocently. "Tracy's always playing with my toys, reading my books, sitting on my bed and combing her hair with my comb. Now it'll be easy for her to remember to stay out of my things!"

Quietly, Mrs. Anderson picked up a black magic marker from the desk. On a few of Melissa's labels she crossed out her daughter's name and wrote in God's name. Melissa nodded sheepishly. In her desire to keep Tracy out of her things, she had forgotten just who really owned all her possessions.

Just like Melissa, we often find it hard to share with others what we own. Sharing might come more easily if we remember that we are only taking care of God's good gifts for him. God gives us possessions to make us happy, but he also wants us to share these gifts with others. Not only do our toys, books, and bikes belong to God, but all the things we can't see do too, including our time, energy, and talents. Have you been asked lately to help out around the house, watch a younger brother, or to finish your homework? Have you done so without complaint? When we remember God is the giver of our health and our very life, we will want to answer "yes" to the requests that are made of us.

As sinners, however, our "yeses" don't come as easily as they should. Satan is constantly rubbing out God's name from our gifts and substituting our name, or his name instead—as if he or we were the real owners. This seems to be especially true of the money in our pockets. As sinful human beings, we often are tempted to keep our money for ourselves. This holds true even when we are asked to give to our church. We know in our hearts that, if it weren't for God, we'd be penniless. Yet, money is often the hardest gift for us to give freely.

But the *duty* of giving turns into the *privilege* of giving much more readily when we remember Christ's suffering and death on the cross. When Jesus was cruelly nailed to the rough wood on Calvary's cross, he took from us the only thing we ever truly owned: our sins. On that cross he rubbed out every sinner's name from God's huge list of debts and debtors and wrote in his own name. He paid his Father in full for what had been demanded of us.

174

Give so this good news of Jesus' forgiveness can be spread around. Give so that more and more will be added to those being saved.

Prayer: Dear Heavenly Father, how hard it is to share what you have so richly given to me. Remind me constantly how unselfish your son was to die that cruel death on the cross in my place. Help me to give as you have given to me. Amen.

God's Way of Starting Over With Us

In reply Jesus declared, "I tell you the truth, no one can see the kingdom of God unless he is born again." (John 3:3)

Lindsay's mouth dropped open in surprise. Through the kitchen window she could see baby Justin tumbling playfully in the wet, muddy grass with Buffy, the neighbor's little dog. Justin's freshly-washed clothes were spattered with thick, gooey mud. His hair was a tangle of wet leaves, and his white baby shoes were the furthest thing from the color they used to be.

"Justin!" Lindsay scolded. "Did you turn on the hose? Who let the dog out? And who took you out of your playpen?" she cried, running across the lawn to scoop him up. She didn't expect an answer from the baby, but asked the questions out of frustration. She suddenly realized that she was carrying on a conversation only with herself.

Jason politely opened the door for his sister as she carefully set their muddy cousin on the doormat. "Honestly, Lindsay, I think it would be easier to start over with a new baby than to clean this one up!" he grinned.

"Start over?" Lindsay cried, as she filled the sink with soapy water. "Stop kidding around. You couldn't part with this bundle of mischief if you tried!" she smiled.

Mrs. Anderson popped her head through the doorway as Lindsay lowered little Justin into the soapsuds. She rumpled Jason's hair and smiled. "As ridiculous as your idea sounded to Lindsay, this is exactly what God did to us at our baptism. In a real way, he started over with us."

"But after we were baptized, we didn't look any different," Jason answered.

"Still, we were changed completely. Being baptized is like being born all over again. Remember the story of Nicodemus?" Mom asked.

"Sure, Nicodemus was a Pharisee who knew about Jesus' teaching and miracles, yet he was not sure about Jesus. He did believe that he was a teacher sent by God. But he did not yet believe Jesus was truly God's Son and the Savior of the world," Jason answered.

"Jesus told him that no one could enter God's kingdom, unless he was born again," Lindsay added. "Jesus was talking about the miracle of baptism."

"When we are baptized, do we become a different person, even though we look the same?" asked Jason.

"Yes, when water is applied in the name of the triune God, the Holy Spirit enters our hearts and creates faith. Before baptism we all are children of the devil, but when we are baptized we begin to trust in God's forgiveness. Baptism is like being born again, a complete starting over," Mom explained.

"What happens if we sin again, after becoming God's child? Is there any way God makes us clean again, the way Lindsay washed the mud off little Justin? Should we be baptized again?"

"No, our baptism lasts our entire lifetime, but because we continue to sin, God wants us to use our baptism by daily confessing our sins and trusting in Jesus' forgiveness. Our sorrow over sins, worked by his power in us, shows that we truly want to give up our sins and live each day for Jesus. God also promises he will give us the strength to turn our backs on the devil's temptations."

Lindsay lifted Justin out of the sink and wrapped a warm towel around him. "Clean on the outside!" she said, rubbing her nose against his, "to match the clean on the inside!" She squeezed him lovingly, trusting he was truly clean because of his baptism.

Prayer: Dear Jesus, I know my sin has made my heart very dirty, and I am not always willing to act as you want me to. Thank you for changing my heart and making me your child through baptism. Amen.

Our Talents—Bragged, Buried, Or Used?

Well done, good and faithful servant! You have been faithful with a few things; I will put you in charge of many things. Come and share your master's happiness! (Matthew 25:21)

"One hundred and fifty. That's what my IQ is!" Michael boasted to his sister one evening. "Look, it says so in this letter from school."

"I don't think you were supposed to open that letter," Melissa scolded. She looked over her brother's shoulder. "But if your IQ is high, mine will be, too, since we're twins."

"I'm afraid not," Michael answered, pointing to his sister's name on the sheet. "Don't worry, at least you still have your looks," he teased.

Melissa looked sadly at the number behind her name. Her IQ was a whole thirty points below her brother's.

"One hundred fifty is probably your bragging score, Michael," Lindsay scolded, patting her sister on the back. "Instead of opening Mom and Dad's mail, you'd better read this." Lindsay tossed Michael a small sheet of yellow paper.

"My grades for this quarter!" he gasped. "Has Dad seen them yet?"

"He certainly has," Mr. Anderson answered sternly from the doorway. "I think you owe us an explanation for these low grades."

Michael fumbled. "They aren't so bad, Dad. At least I didn't fail."

"But with your high IQ we expect A's and B's on your report card. I can assure you, young man, that this next quarter has a lot of hard work in store for you!"

Michael loved to boast about his intelligence, even to the point of making his sister feel sad and foolish. Later, he learned Melissa had nothing to be ashamed of. By hard work she had earned the grades her father expected of him. Mr. Anderson had to remind Michael that his high intelligence was a gift from God and, therefore, he had no right to boast. He soon discovered his high IQ didn't mean he could relax and take life easy. Now, his teachers and parents expected even more of him.

Are you burying your talents? When the master in this parable came home, he discovered that one of his servants had wasted the money which he had been given. Instead of investing the money, he had buried it. Because of his unfaithfulness, the money was given to the servant who had used his wisely. Not to use God's gifts results in losing them.

Are you wasting your talents, or blaming God for not giving you any? Be careful! Simple laziness may be keeping you from finding and using your talents. Perhaps God has made you very smart! Or perhaps he has given you the ability to speak fluently or to draw well or to play an instrument or to excel at a certain sport. Whatever talent you have, God expects you to put it to work, to use it for the benefit of his kingdom. It may take sweat and labor on your part to perfect your skills. But even then we must humbly admit they were God's gifts to us in the first place. Instead of bragging, we'll want to give all credit to God.

Prayer: Dear Jesus, forgive my laziness and boasting. Everything I do well I do because of you. Keep my faith strong so I may willingly put my talents to use in serving you. Amen.

Getting Even

When they hurled their insults at him, he did not retaliate; when he suffered, he made no threats. Instead, he entrusted himself to him who judges justly. **(1 Peter 2:23)**

Jason Anderson and Brian Mitchell stood at the doors of their lockers, whispering excitedly. "Have you figured out how to get back at Keith Rogers for what he did yesterday?" asked Brian.

Jason nodded and laughed loudly, remembering what Keith had done the day before. Keith had fixed the water cooler so that whoever turned it on to get a drink would be sprayed from head to toe. Jason had spent an uncomfortable afternoon in his drenched clothing. Today Keith would feel the sting of Jason's revenge.

Most of the Junior High kids were filing out of the cafeteria on their way to class. Keith was in the lead as usual. Jason's plan seemed foolproof. Unexpectedly, however, Principal Filmore appeared from the opposite corner. He would quickly snatch a drink before the long line of thirsty students.

Jason and Brian gasped as the spray of water shot into the air. It soaked the principal. Mr. Filmore's eyes blazed with anger as water dripped from his hair and face and spotted his neatly pressed suit. He pulled his handkerchief from his pocket to wipe his dripping brow.

Getting even with Keith had back-fired. Three hours later, Jason found himself in Mr. Filmore's office with a cramped hand. He had almost completed the thousand-word essay he had been assigned. And for the next two weeks he'd be sitting in detention hall.

When someone has played a trick on us, it's hard to sit back quietly and not try to get even. One way or another we want to pay that person back. Jason wanted to show Keith how it felt to be sprayed with cold water from the drinking fountain and sit in soaked clothing for the rest of the day. In the end, however, Keith wasn't punished at all. Instead, Jason found himself in deep trouble with the principal.

Was there a better solution? Praying for someone who has made fun of us is certainly difficult. If it seems hard for us to do, remember how fervently Jesus begs his Father every day to have mercy on us. He reminds his Father that he has already paid for our sins with his death on the cross. Because of Jesus' love we are forgiven. Because of Jesus' love we too will forgive.

Paying back? Nothing's easier. Forgiving so completely— that's the tough part!

Prayer: Dear Jesus, when someone makes fun of me or makes me look foolish, it's hard to keep from getting even. Remind me then of how much you suffered to forgive my sins. Help me in turn to be kind, even to those who don't like me. Amen.

Except Jesus Christ And Him Crucified

For I resolved to know nothing while I was with you except Jesus Christ and him crucified. (1 Corinthians 2:2)

"How was Sunday School?" asked Dad when the Anderson family sat down to the roast chicken dinner. Tracy giggled and immediately began to sing the tune and act out the words of the new song about Zaccheus which she had learned in her class.

Jason smiled when his sister was finished. "We had the story of Zaccheus, too," he explained. "The Bible lesson was interesting, but afterwards Miss Grant spent so much time

talking about Jesus' dying for our sins. After all, we just heard about all those events during Lent and Easter."

"Well, Jason," Mom remarked, "she stresses Jesus' death and suffering because it was the way he saved us from our sins."

"But, Mom, we know how we've been saved. How many times does she have to repeat it? Why doesn't she teach us about other things?"

"What other things could be more important?" asked Dad.

"Well, since the story was all about Zaccheus, we should have talked more about stealing. I mean, she mentioned it and we discussed it a little, but then we went right back to hammering away about Jesus' death on the cross. Why doesn't she stick to the main story?"

"But, Jason," Dad explained, "all the stories in the Bible revolve around Jesus' life. We should want to be like the apostle Paul who told the Corinthian Christians, 'I resolved to know nothing while I was with you, except Jesus Christ and him crucified.' "

"What about all the faults our teacher could be helping us change?" asked Jason. "Emily Swit is constantly gossiping about someone; Jeremy Campbell can't take a test without cheating, and every other sentence John Hall speaks is a lie."

"You see, Jason, no matter how much we drill the do's and don'ts, sinful human beings continue to disobey the commandments. They are simply unable to keep them perfectly."

"Only Jesus has the power to be perfect," Melissa helped.

"This is the reason we want to keep stressing how Jesus

181

has saved us," Mom explained. "The law only condemns us and shows us just how imperfect we are. It is the gospel of Jesus which moves us to do what God asks of us. Only after having the gospel, can we look upon the law to guide us in the way to thank Jesus."

"With faith in Christ as the Savior, we can live a pleasing life to God. Only Emily's love for her Savior will make her want to stop gossiping. Cheating, lying, stealing, and even murder will be willingly put away, out of thankfulness for God's great love for us."

"Is it our sinfulness which makes the story of Jesus monotonous and boring to us?" asked Lindsay.

Dad nodded. "Our sinful nature always wants to try to live perfectly without Jesus. The devil, too, wants us to think we have enough power on our own to keep the commandments and earn our way to heaven."

Jason nodded meekly. "I completely forgot, too, about all the visitors who come to our class. It may be the only time they'll ever hear about Jesus and how he saved us."

The story of Jesus—we know it so well! Has it lost the sparkle and excitement it once had when you first heard it? Could our senses be growing dull to the great good news that Jesus' suffering and death saved us from the fires of hell, from eternal damnation, from a permanent separation from God? Have we forgotten how the devil walks around like a roaring lion looking for a Christian whom he can persuade to sin? Let us run to the story which closes the mouth of that dread lion and which extinguishes the fires of hell for us. How can we grow tired of being saved from such things and saved for the great glory which shall be ours because of Christ Jesus?

Prayer: I love to tell the story of unseen things above. Of Jesus and his glory, of Jesus and his love. I love to tell the story, because I know it's true. It satisfies my longing like nothing else can do. I love to tell the story, will be my theme in glory—to tell the old, old story of Jesus and his love.

182

The Heart Of Prayer

These people honor me with their lips, but their hearts are far from me. (Matthew 15:8)

Lindsay Anderson sat on Melissa's bed. Her brothers and sisters knelt in a row beside the other bed. From the youngest to the oldest, each child said his prayers. When they were through, Lindsay smiled approvingly and stood up to tuck the little ones in their beds. To her surprise, Michael began his prayers again.

"Dear Jesus, please forgive me all my sins. Bless Daddy and . . ."

"Michael," Melissa interrupted her brother with an impatient poke. "You've already said your prayers."

Michael looked up, bewildered. "I did? I don't remember."

"You don't remember?" hooted Jason. "You just said them no more than five minutes ago."

Michael faltered. "Are you sure? I thought you skipped me."

Lindsay sighed and sat down once again. "You'd better say them again if you don't really remember."

When Michael had finished the second time, his cheeks were red with embarrassment. "My mind must have wandered before, but now I'm positive I said them," he grinned.

"Maybe saying them double will help you get an answer," Tracy put in.

"No, Tracy," Lindsay answered quickly. "It's not the rattling off of words that makes a prayer. We have to *think about* the words we say and speak them from the *heart*. That's what matters to God."

Melissa nodded. "Mom told me praying isn't like reciting a bunch of magic words. Prayer is as real as speaking into the receiver of a telephone. The only difference is that God answers us back in many different ways. One of the ways he answers is through his word."

"The Bible?" Michael asked, puzzled. "But when I ask for a new skateboard, how can the Bible tell me whether or not I'll get it?"

Lindsay smiled. "It is true, the Bible doesn't have much to say on the subject of skateboards, Michael, but you may still be surprised to know the answer is there."

"Where will I find it?" asked Michael, still puzzled.

"God's opinion on skateboards and everything else we ask for is found in the passage, "If we ask anything according to his will, he hears us" (1 John 5:13).

"So, if it is God's will for you to have a skateboard, he'll give it to you," Jason finished.

"But if God knows it would mean a lot of broken bones for you, he may decide it's not so good for you," Lindsay reminded him.

"And you can't expect to receive anything from God if you don't even think about the words you are saying," Melissa reminded her twin brother.

"Believe me, I'll never be so absent-minded again."

"We are the only ones who lose when we don't put our hearts into our prayers," Lindsay added. "There isn't a thing we can get on our own in this world without God's help."

"Especially the forgiveness of sins," Jason replied thoughtfully.

"And a stronger faith and life in heaven," Melissa added.

"Those are the blessings that God wants us to especially ask for. We know they are what we need for our souls."

"And they are ours, just for the asking!" Tracy exclaimed.

"But always asking from the heart," Michael grinned.

Prayer: Dear Jesus, sometimes I forget to say my prayers, and sometimes I forget to think about the words I am saying. Forgive me for praying without thinking. Only you can give me forgiveness and everything I need to live. Amen.

Your Gospel Statement

But [Jesus] made himself nothing, taking the very nature of a servant, being made in human likeness. And being found in appearance as a man, he humbled himself and became obedient to death—even death on a cross! (Philippians 2:7,8)

Carol studied the pile of birthday invitations setting on the Anderson's dining room table. "Teresa Wilson?" she squeaked. "Melissa, you aren't thinking of inviting her to your birthday party, are you?"

"Why not? She sits next to me in math. I like her."

"Math is one thing, but a birthday party is a social statement! You don't want the daughter of a garbage collector attending your party."

"There's nothing wrong with collecting garbage," Jason interrupted the girls. "It's one of the highest-paying jobs in the city! What a social statement it would make having your trash laying all over your yard," he added with a smirk.

"What do you boys know?" sniffed Carol, grabbing her coat. "Take it from me, Melissa, you'd be doing Teresa a favor by not inviting her. She wouldn't know how to act around lace tablecloths and fancy china."

"Something wrong?" Mom asked, after Carol had left.

"Oh, I thought I had my whole party planned, especially the guest list. Now Carol says I shouldn't invite Teresa because her dad is a garbage collector."

"What do you think?" asked Mom.

"I think it shouldn't matter where her father works, but I know I'm in the minority. Some kids won't be seen with other kids who don't meet their standards."

"I hope you won't encourage their way of thinking," Mom answered. "How dare any of us think we are better than anyone else? We are all sinners in need of a Savior."

"I wonder if Jesus had to face this problem when he was young," Melissa sighed.

"I'm sure he did," Mom answered. "When he was beginning his public ministry, the Pharisees of his day expected him only to associate with the people they considered respectable."

"But Jesus wanted to show he was the Savior of all people, that he had come into the world to save sinners."

Mom nodded. "He looked into hearts, searching for the real treasure of faith there instead of wealth or family position or outward goodness."

"If Jesus wasn't ashamed of anyone, neither should I be," Melissa decided. "I'm going to invite Teresa, even if it means social suicide." She licked the envelope emphatically.

"Hey, Melissa," Lindsay called. "I'm heading out to the mailbox. Are your birthday invitations ready?" With a smile, Melissa handed them to her sister. The top envelope caught Lindsay's eye. "Teresa Wilson? I know her sister. We ride the bus together every day to her dad's office."

"Her dad has his own office?" asked Melissa in surprise.

Lindsay blinked. "Doctors usually do, don't they?"

"Her dad is a doctor?" asked Melissa. "Carol said he collected garbage."

Lindsay looked puzzled. Finally her eyes brightened. "Oh, Dr. Wilson's been helping a sick friend with his sanitation business. It seems he put himself through medical school shoveling trash. Highest paying job in the city, you know."

"So I've heard," Melissa grinned, watching her sister leave with the invitations. She turned to Mom. "I'm glad Teresa's envelope was already sealed, because garbage collector or doctor, I know in my heart it never really mattered."

Prayer: Dear Jesus, I am sorry for thinking I am sometimes better than another person. Help me to remember all I have I owe to you alone. Give me the courage to make a gospel statement by befriending others, even those who are looked down upon. Amen.

Like A Tower Of Babel

Instead, you ought to say, "If it is the Lord's will, we will live and do this or that." (James 4:15)

"Citizens Realty has offered me a promotion," Dad declared one night at the supper table. "It will mean higher pay, and I will be managing twice as many people as I am managing now. It is clearly a step up. But," Dad hesitated, "this job is on the West Coast. It means we would have to move."

Silence hovered over the table as the family swallowed their food along with Dad's unusual announcement. When they realized how this could change all their lives, the table came to life with loud, excited voices.

"Maybe we'd get to live in a bigger house! With a pool! We could take trips to the ocean! And trips to Disneyland!"

"But keep in mind that we'd be leaving friends behind, church friends as well as school friends," Mom reminded them all. "A move like this is a big step, one that we'll have to consider with much thought and prayer."

"It is a big step," Jason agreed, "but if Dad wants to climb the corporate ladder of success, he must never turn down a promotion! Everyone knows that is corporate suicide."

Dad's eyes twinkled softly as he listened to his son's reasoning. "We planned a vacation with the same thought in mind when your mom and I were first married."

Mom's eyes suddenly turned bright with laughter. "Lindsay was just a baby. Dad and I decided we simply needed a month's vacation on the West Coast. For a whole year we scrimped and saved."

"There's nothing wrong with planning and saving," Jason said.

"No, except our planning and saving never included asking God's direction or blessing. We saw an opportunity to go and we went," Dad answered.

"Our car broke down in an out of the way place in New Mexico. We spent most of our beautiful vacation in a cheap, hot motel, waiting for the part the mechanic needed for our car," Mom continued.

"All of our beautiful plans went up in smoke. It was then we made a promise to God never to start anything without praying that his will be done," Dad finished.

"How will we know if it is God's will to move or not?" asked Lindsay.

"We'll make a list of all the reasons we should move and all the reasons we should stay. We'll ask questions such as: Is there a church of our fellowship nearby? Does it have a Christian grade school and high school? Is the city's environment one which will help or hinder our growing faith?"

"Would a bigger salary and a better position be a good reason to move?" Jason asked hopefully.

"Those could be legitimate reasons," Dad agreed. "We have a large family and we would like to educate all of you. Yet, the spiritual needs of our family still come first."

"If we don't remember Jesus in our plans, we could be just like those people who built the Tower of Babel," Lindsay said.

"Yes, we could be," Dad replied. "God destroyed the tower because it wasn't built to honor him. Those people only built it to show what great things man could achieve. Instead of building a monument to themselves, God wanted them to confess their sins and look for forgiveness through the promised Savior he would send one day."

With folded hands, the Anderson family sought God's guidance in their decision to move west.

As you grow older and face new opportunities and challenges, may you also begin with prayer.

Prayer: Dear Jesus, I ask for your guidance in my life. May your will always be done. Remind me that my spiritual needs should come before all others. Amen.

A Lesson Of The Plant

Bear with each other and forgive whatever grievances you may have against one another. Forgive as the Lord forgave you. **(Colossians 3:13)**

"Something wrong?" asked Mom, noticing Melissa's angry scowl.

"Oh, Melissa's angry about Willie Corbin, the guy who slashed all those bike tires at school," Michael answered.

"Willie was supposed to be expelled, but now they decided to give him a second chance," Melissa replied angrily.

"Are you angry because he didn't get what he deserved?" asked Mom.

"Sure I am," Melissa answered. "He gets to come to school, while my bike sits in the garage, practically dead."

"This situation sounds to me a little bit like the story of Jonah," Mom began, placing a plate of raw vegetables before her children.

"Did Jonah ruin bikes, too?" asked little Tracy.

Mom smiled. "No, but he knew some people living in the city of Ninevah who were very wicked. God wanted to bring them to feel sorry for their sins."

"Jonah didn't want to go," Michael continued. "He didn't think they deserved a chance to repent. He wanted God to destroy them."

"Do you think Jonah knew these people first-hand, like I know Willie?" Melissa asked.

"It is possible, but we don't really know," Mom replied. "At any rate, Jonah disobeyed God. In fact, rather than going to Ninevah as God wanted him to, he took a ship in the opposite direction. He didn't want to perform the work which the Lord had given him to do."

"Yes, now I remember," Tracy answered. "A big fish gulped Jonah right down." She swallowed a handful of frozen peas dramatically.

"After being in the fish for three days, Jonah begged God to help him. He finally agreed to go and preach to Ninevah. The problem was that Jonah's attitude still hadn't changed too much. Even after he preached his message of repentance, he sat outside the city and waited for God to destroy it. As he watched and waited, he became very hot. God allowed a huge vine to grow up very quickly to give him shade. Jonah was very happy for it made it much cooler for him. Suddenly a worm attacked the vine, and it withered and died. Now Jonah was angrier and sadder than ever! His lovely shade was gone," Mom said.

"Jonah was sad about the dead plant, but he wasn't sad to see a whole city destroyed," Michael concluded. "A city is worth much more than a plant."

"Yes," Mom nodded. "That was the lesson God tried to teach Jonah: that we should be concerned about lost souls, those without Christ and without hope in the world."

"Did Jonah's preaching help? Did Ninevah repent?" asked Michael.

Mom nodded and smiled. "What a blessing, God gave them a second chance."

Melissa smiled, too. "I can give Willie a second chance, too. He is more important than bike tires."

"Then, I think you are ready to read this," Mom answered.

With a puzzled look, Melissa accepted the small note her mother handed her.

190

Dear Melissa,

I am sending you an IOU for two new bike tires. I will pay you back when I earn enough money. I was afraid the kids wouldn't believe how sorry I am, but I know you will.

Your classmate, Willie

"It'll take Willie the rest of his life to pay everyone back, Michael gasped. "Have you any idea how much sixty bike tires cost?"

"Fifty-eight bike tires," Melissa corrected him. With bold strokes she printed. "Paid in Full" over Willie's letter. She handed it to her mother. "Would you mail this?" she grinned, "before a huge vine starts growing beside *my* bedroom window?"

Prayer: Dear Jesus, forgive me when I'm unwilling to give others a second chance when they hurt me. Remind me of your forgiveness won for me on the cross. Amen.

I'm So Worried

If you make the Most High your dwelling—even the LORD, who is my refuge—then no harm will befall you, no disaster will come near your tent. (Psalm 91:9,10)

Tracy gathered her Barbies all around her, arranging and rearranging the tiny bed, table, and chairs in various positions. Melissa rocked back on her heels, frowning impatiently. "When are you going to start playing?" she asked. "Should we dress the Barbies in swimming suits, pajamas, or evening dresses?"

Tracy shrugged. "We might as well dress them for moving," she answered bitterly.

Melissa softened. "Are you still worried about moving to our new house?"

". . . and a new neighborhood and a new school," Tracy sighed loudly. "If we move, I'll lose all my good friends. If I lose all my good friends, I may not make any new ones. If I don't make any new ones, my grades will be terrible in first grade. I may never learn to read. If I can't read, I'll have to be put back, which might make me feel like dropping out of school altogether. And what kind of a job can a grade school drop-out get these days?"

Melissa stared at her little sister in surprise. "You worry too much, Tracy. I mean, the world may end before Mom calls you to supper. Try taking life minute by minute, would you?"

Tracy sighed. "Aren't you just a little worried about moving?"

"Once in a while I get a little panicky. I wonder if everything will be okay. Then, I think of all the other times God has taken care of us."

Tracy closed her eyes and thought. "Do you mean like last summer when Jason pulled me from the lake after I slipped off the dock?"

"Or the time the car door opened and you fell onto the pavement," Melissa answered.

"Or the time Michael climbed up to the garage roof for a ball and slipped off, but only sprained his knee?" Tracy asked.

"Or the time the deep fat fryer fell on the floor, and Mom only burned her thumb picking up the hot pan," Melissa added. "Two or three of us could be in a coffin right now for all the accidents and mishaps our family has gone through."

"Is that why you aren't worried about moving?" asked Tracy. "Is it because God has always taken care of us before?"

"Yes, except those aren't the main reasons. Even if all those accidents would have ended badly, I still would know I could trust Jesus to take care of us."

"Because of Christmas, Good Friday, and Easter," Melissa replied. "If Jesus cared enough about me to give up his life for me, I am positive he loves me. I'm sure he'll be watching out for me even in a far away place like California. Even if a few things go wrong, I know Jesus is watching out for my soul. He'll keep it safe until I go to heaven."

Tracy looked down at her Barbies. She silently selected one of her newest outfits and began to dress the doll. "Well, what are you waiting for, Melissa? Get these dolls dressed. Haven't you heard? We're moving to California." Tracy paused. "You know, it doesn't hurt to get a little excited," she crowed, as her eyes twinkled brightly.

Prayer: Dear Jesus, forgive me for worrying. Help me to realize you are with me wherever I go and that you will watch over my soul. Amen.

Thanksgiving Inventory

Always giving thanks to God the Father for everything, in the name of our Lord Jesus Christ. (Ephesians 5:20)

"In-vent-what?" Jason asked his sister, who stood with him in the cosmetic department of Uncle Fred's Drug Store.

"In-ven-tory" Lindsay explained. "Here is what you do. Write down each item on this clipboard and put its code number beside it. Then write in the price. Taking inventory isn't hard; it's just very time-consuming."

Jason set his jaw and headed for the nail polish. "How could one lady wear all this stuff in a lifetime?" he asked after he had spent a few minutes counting containers.

Lindsay laughed heartily. "It is unbelievable how much Uncle Fred needs to supply his shop."

"Why does Uncle Fred have to have a record of all these items?"

"He needs them for tax purposes. He has to pay a tax on everything in the store."

"No wonder people are always so gloomy during inventory time," Jason answered.

"Not Uncle Fred! He calls inventory time his Thanksgiving time. He is thankful to have a store to pay taxes on. His business is quite successful."

"Mmmm," answered Jason. "This gives me a good idea for my Thanksgiving essay for school. I'll take my own inventory at home to see just what I have to be thankful for!"

The next day, Jason's head was buried under several papers piled on his desk. Lindsay bent over his shoulder to inspect his inventory.

"I think you've overpriced your toothbrush!" Lindsay laughed.

Jason smiled. "At least this part of my inventory was easy; I can always come up with a price for what my possessions are worth. Take my bedspread, for instance. I said it was worth about thirty dollars. But there are certain things like my life, parents, brothers, and sisters which are hard to place a price tag on."

Lindsay gazed at the sheet Jason was working on. "A million dollars?" she squealed, reading the amount behind her name. "Am I really worth a million dollars to you?"

"When something is worth a lot, the price just naturally must go up," he answered shyly. "But there is still one item I couldn't price. I couldn't come up with a price for Jesus' death on the cross which paid for my sins. No number seems high enough."

Lindsay thought for a minute. "I don't think God would want us to put a price on Jesus' love for us. It's priceless."

"Should I leave that space blank then?" asked Jason.

"Maybe you don't have to," she answered. "Remember how Uncle Fred called Inventory Days his real thanksgiving? Well, why not write the words THANK YOU in the space after Jesus' name?"

"Hey, of course," Jason answered. "Pastor Miles is always telling us our whole life should be a thank-you to Jesus for suffering for us."

194

Thanksgiving is a special time when we say thank you to God for all the gifts he has given us. But we could never enjoy any of these earthly gifts if Jesus hadn't paid for our sins. We no longer have any guilt hanging over our heads.

God has showered us with so many treasures. Jesus, our Savior, is our highest treasure. We could never put a price on what he has done for us. May he be at the very top of our "Thanksgiving Inventory."

Prayer: Jesus, priceless Treasure, fount of purest pleasure, Truest Friend to me. Ah, how long in anguish Shall my spirit languish, Yearning, Lord, for Thee? Thou art mine, O Lamb divine! I will suffer naught to hide Thee, Naught I ask beside thee. (TLH 347:1)

Songs Of Thankfulness And Praise

Give thanks to the LORD, for he is good; his love endures forever. (Psalm 118:1)

The Anderson children tumbled into their chairs ready for their early morning breakfast. After they prayed, Mom dished the food onto plates, and the family hungrily began to eat.

Michael took one bite of his scrambled eggs and dropped his fork in disgust. "These eggs are just lukewarm, Mom."

"Yours must have been dished up first," Lindsay explained to her brother. She spread a huge coating of peanut butter over her toast. "I wish you would have bought creamy peanut butter, Mom. This crunchy kind gets stuck between my teeth!"

"And how come the raspberry jam doesn't have seeds in it?" complained Melissa. "It tastes like jelly instead of jam!"

"Mommy, is it all right if I don't eat my toast?" asked Tracy. "My piece is so brown it's almost burnt!" She wriggled her nose to show how she felt about it.

Jason was about to open his mouth, when Mrs. Anderson rose from the table. She quickly gathered up the unfinished plates of food. The children's mouths dropped open as she whisked everything off the table.

"Mom, I wasn't finished," Michael cried as he held the tablecloth down tightly, hoping Mom wouldn't take that, too!

"I still want more toast," Melissa chimed in.

"Mom wants to make an impression on you," Dad began. "I think that is the reason she took all of your food away. Ever since you began to eat, all you've done is to complain about the food. Perhaps it would help if we began this meal again," Dad suggested solemnly. "But this time let's begin with our *thank you* prayer, rather than waiting to end with it. Instead of complaining while we eat, let's remember to be thankful we've got something *to* eat!"

Do your mealtimes sometimes sound similar to the Anderson's breakfast table? In our country we are blessed with more food, clothing, and luxuries than any other country in the world. Sad to say, the richest country in the world is also filled with some of the worst complainers.

If every single one of our possessions were snatched away from us, perhaps then we'd be grateful just to get our hands on a crust of bread to fill our empty stomachs. Perhaps then our eyes would fill with tears of thankfulness if we'd receive a ragged coat to keep out the winter's chill.

How important it is to be thankful for God's gifts to us! Everything we own belongs to God. Out of love he provides for all our needs, and he even provides us with things we don't need. And most important, out of love God sent his Son Jesus to die on the cross for our sins that we might inherit heaven!

Let us not forget what we were before Jesus gave up his life for us. We were the most miserable creatures! We were loathsome to God, covered with sin, and headed straight for hell. Instead of destroying us as we deserved, God forgave our sins. He covered our filthiness with Jesus' goodness. Instead of complaining, let us with joyful hearts thank God for his loving gifts, especially the most precious gift of all, his Son, our Savior.

Prayer: Dear Jesus, forgive my complaining. Help me to see how richly you have blessed me. Thank you for giving your life for me on the cross. I will praise you forever for this richest of your gifts. Amen.

Growing Out Of Christmas?

Today in the town of David a Savior has been born to you; he is Christ the Lord. (Luke 2:11)

Melissa Anderson hurried into the kitchen with paper and pencils. Michael, her twin brother, heaved the huge Christmas catalog onto the table. The children sat down quickly and began to write furiously.

"Mom's going shopping this afternoon for Christmas gifts," Melissa told her older brother Jason, who sat down beside her. "We've already memorized what we want," she laughed, "so you can use the catalog in a minute!"

Jason remembered how last year, he, too, had carefully written out the list of toys he wanted for Christmas. This year that seemed like kid's stuff. "I'm too big for that," he sighed, noticing Mom look up at him from the pot of simmering meat she was stirring.

It was true. In the past year Jason had noticed his interests were changing. Only when Michael begged him repeatedly would he get down on his hands and knees and play with cars and trucks. Now he enjoyed listening to the radio or playing football with his friends. Silently, Jason withdrew to his bedroom. Had he outgrown Christmas too?

In a few minutes, Mom appeared at his door. "Is anything wrong?" she asked, noticing the huge cardboard box at his feet filled with old toys and comic books.

"Not really," he sighed. "I decided to clean out my room. There's stuff here I never use any more. Maybe Michael would like my old racing set or a few of these games."

As she turned to leave, Jason asked, "Mom, why do I feel differently about Christmas? I used to go wild, waiting for the tree to be put up and the presents to be tucked underneath. This year I didn't even feel like making out a Christmas list. What is happening to me?"

"When you were little, Dad and I were careful to teach you that Christmas was more than toys under a tree. Even as a toddler you knew Christmas was the birth of God's Son into the world. I think, as we grow older, we realize even more fully that presents don't give lasting happiness. Only our Savior Jesus, who took away all of our sins, gives true peace."

Jason nodded. "Remember the Christmas when I had just turned five? One of my presents was a hook-and-ladder truck. I couldn't wait to tear the wrapping away and play with it. It's funny how excited I got over something which is now gathering dust in my closet."

Mom laughed and nodded. "Even though toys don't excite you any more, Christmas doesn't have to be less exciting. Now you are old enough to open your Bible and study for yourself the marvelous events which led up to Jesus' birth. You can think about how humble Jesus made himself when he was born as a man and how God loved us sinful people!"

Just then, Lindsay appeared at the door. "Want to come over to church with me and help the Sunday School children learn passages for the Christmas service?"

Jason nodded as his eyes grew bright. Being older also meant teaching younger children about the Savior's birth. Those Old Testament passages foretelling Jesus' birth were still stored in his memory, and the unforgettable words of the Christmas story were sealed in his heart. Now Jason knew, for sure, that growing older didn't mean growing out of Christmas. He was old enough to discover for himself just how deep a meaning Christmas has for all sinners!

Prayer: Dear Jesus, as I grow up and begin to see Christmas from a different angle, help my faith also to grow up. Help me to treasure your birth and forgiveness of my sins more than ever. Amen.

Sometimes I Get So Sick Of Cute!

For in Christ all the fullness of the Deity lives in bodily form. (Colossians 2:9)

Lindsay was lying on her bed, staring solemnly up at the ceiling. Mr. Anderson took a seat beside his daughter. "Mom says you've been quiet all afternoon. I'm sure your ceiling isn't much of a conversationalist. Want to try your dear old dad?"

Lindsay smiled. "We had our last children's Sunday School practice today," she began.

"And do the children know their parts?" asked Dad. "You've been working pretty hard helping Mrs. Wadsworth teach them their songs and passages."

"Oh, Dad you should hear them. Even the little ones know the words by heart!" Lindsay replied. Suddenly her enthusiasm soured. "But today's practice turned into a disaster! A few of the children's parents stayed to watch. Little Tommy Meyer's mother was impossible! Every time he opened his mouth, she laughed. It didn't matter that he wasn't saying anything funny. She went into hysterics! It was contagious, too. Soon every mother and child in the place were laughing. They turned so many weeks of worthwhile work into one big joke!"

"Isn't Tommy cute? Oh, look at Jenny! She is just adorable!" Lindsay mimicked a few of the comments she had heard that afternoon. "Oh, Dad, sometimes I get so sick of cute!"

Dad's eyes twinkled merrily as he listened to his oldest daughter's complaints. "Oh, I think God may have had a real purpose in mind when he made children cute. Their babyish faces turn any burden that a parent might feel in caring for them into joy."

"I know, Dad, they are all so precious. But even though they are little, they are speaking God's word, and they do have something important to say!"

Dad nodded seriously. "You are so right, Lindsay. Cuteness isn't going to get anyone to heaven. I suppose God must feel the same way you do when people celebrate Jesus' birthday. To many, Christmas is just a time to get all sentimental about a cute little baby born many years ago in a manger. Many forget this baby is fully God, come to earth in bodily form."

"I suppose we could put bags over the children's heads so no one would be distracted by how cute they are," Lindsay said with a wry smile. "Their parents would have to listen to their words then!"

Dad smiled. "I'm sure your concern is also our pastor's concern every Sunday morning. He prays that his clever introductions and interesting stories will in no way distract from the message of the Bible. He, too, wants people to be attracted to the real preaching of law and gospel, not to his energetic preaching ability. After all, it's God who is our Savior. The preacher is just his humble servant bringing the message."

"So," Dad continued, "instead of putting bags over the children's heads, let us also pray the precious words of God will fall on believing hearts, no matter how cute the speakers are. Many people will come on Christmas Eve who normally don't step inside a church all year long. God's word, even spoken by tiny children, has power. Let us pray the listeners will come to know and believe through their words, that Jesus is more than a cute baby in a manger. May they come to believe he is, indeed, their Savior from sin!"

DEAR CHILDREN:
MAY GOD BLESS YOUR MESSAGE!

The Best Birthday

The Word became flesh and made his dwelling among us. We have seen his glory, the glory of the One and Only, who came from the Father, full of grace and truth. (John 1:14)

Little Tracy Anderson stood quietly beside the red tablecloth. She watched as her mother let the wet knife slip cleanly through the beautiful, pure, white Christmas cake. "It has been the best Christmas of all!" she told herself. Her eyes glowed with happiness as she remembered how she had recited her entire Christmas verse without a mistake the night before.

Mrs. Anderson smiled and handed her daughter two dessert plates. Carefully, Tracy walked into the living room, handing the pieces of cake to the outstretched hands. The spicy smell of pine caught her attention, and she lingered for a moment beside the Christmas tree. What joy and excitement had rung throughout this very room when each brightly-colored package had been opened.

Hearing her mother's call, she hurried back into the kitchen to finish serving the dessert to her family. Before long every Anderson held a fork and a plate. Tracy bit into the birthday cake and rolled her eyes in delight.

"There isn't any birthday party better than Jesus'!" she declared excitedly.

"Is it even better than Sara Long's birthday party at McDonald's?" asked Melissa, giving her little sister a wink. "You dressed as Cinderella, remember?"

"Oh, McDonald's is hard to beat!" laughed Tracy. "But at Sara's party we all brought the presents to her. At Jesus' birthday everyone gives them all to us! And it's not even *our* birthday."

Jason nodded thoughtfully. "But what would Jesus do with Lindsay's ice skates, or Michael's train set, or Melissa's new dolls?"

"Doesn't Jesus ever like to play?" Tracy asked her father sadly.

His eyes twinkled merrily as he looked down at her. "When Jesus was a young boy, I'm sure he probably played many fine games just like you do."

"But what about now?" asked Michael. "Christmas is Jesus' birthday, and yet we are the ones who get everything nice."

Mom swallowed her last bit of cake and set her plate gently on the coffee table. "It seems to me that is how it always is, not only at Christmas, but all through the year. We are the ones who receive blessing after blessing after blessing."

"We sin and make God sad, then he turns around and forgives us," Dad answered. "And he doesn't just forgive us once, but again and again. Above and beyond all the pretty cards, good food, presents, and beautiful decorations, forgiveness of our sins is the most important gift given to us."

"It is good to be concerned about how God feels on Christmas," Mom added thoughtfully. "It is important to make him happy that we are his children by faith."

"But how do we make God happy?" asked Michael. "He's not interested in toys."

"But he is interested in hearts," Dad replied. "He wants us to come before him with truly sorry hearts, seeking his forgiveness when we sin. He wants us to come before him with believing hearts, believing we are forgiven by Jesus' life, death, and resurrection."

"I don't think I could ever make God as happy as he has made me," Tracy answered. "But if he wants my heart, it's his. After all, he paid for it with his own blood! He can have not just my heart, but every bit of me," she smiled, "because there is no one who loves me as much as he does."

Prayer: Dear Jesus, help me to look beyond all the presents and decorations at Christmas time. Thank you for giving me yourself as my most precious gift. Forgive me all my sins, and help me to trust in you always. Amen.